MAKING

SPACE

MAKING—

PA PRESS

PRINCETON ARCHITECTURAL PRESS · NEW YORK

LILI WEIGERT

—SPACE

ADUs FOR MODERN LIVING

Published by
Princeton Architectural Press
A division of Chronicle Books LLC
70 West 36th Street
New York, NY 10018
papress.com

Printed and bound in China
28 27 26 25   4 3 2 1   First edition

Editor: Jennifer Thompson
Designer: Natalie Snodgrass

Library of Congress Cataloging-in-Publication Data
Names: Weigert, Lili, author.
Title: Making space : ADUs for modern living / Lili Weigert.
Description: New York : Princeton Architectural Press, [2025] | Summary: "A practical exploration of the next generation of ADUs (Accessory Dwelling Units), featuring profiles, essays, and vibrant photography"—Provided by publisher.
Identifiers: LCCN 2024062045 | ISBN 9781797232874 (hardcover) | ISBN 9781797232881 (ebook)
Subjects: LCSH: Small houses. | Infill housing. | Accessory apartments.
Classification: LCC NA7533 .W45 2025 | DDC 728/.37—dc23/eng/20250127
LC record available at https://lccn.loc.gov/2024062045

For Casper, for believing in me and joining me on this journey.

And for Hector and Theo, for keeping me hopeful for the future.

CONTENTS

PREFACE

In California, it seems like every homeowner has either added an Accessory Dwelling Unit (ADU) or is seriously considering it. The first time I heard the term was in 2021, when a friend bought a house near me in Marin County. His property had a large, flat backyard, and he mentioned new legislation that might allow him to build a second unit there. Given California's housing crisis, it made sense that the county would encourage homeowners with extra space to help expand the housing supply.

After that, I started hearing about ADUs everywhere. Building sites listed "ADU construction" among their services, architecture firms began calling themselves "ADU specialists," and builders started incorporating ADUs into new home designs—sometimes instead of a garage.

I've lived in something similar to an ADU, but it was called an earthquake cottage. Hundreds of these were built as temporary housing after the 1906 San Francisco earthquake, intended to shelter people while their homes were rebuilt. They were all supposed to be demolished but a few survived, especially in certain neighborhoods like Bernal Heights and Noe Valley, where I lived. My house was a 630-square-foot box, but it was full of charm. It had two bedrooms when I moved in, but I knocked down some walls to create a more open living and kitchen area. Tucked behind a three-story Edwardian, the cottage was invisible from the street and accessed via a side path, with its own private brick patio. That cottage was the beginning of my interest in small-space living. I learned firsthand that 630 square feet was plenty of space for one person—and, in many ways, living smaller was easier.

With all the buzz around ADUs, I pitched an article for *Marin Magazine*. I interviewed architects, city planners, builders, and real estate agents across the county to understand why ADUs were gaining so much traction. That's when I realized just how big the story was. Bigger than Marin, or even California—it was global.

ADUs aren't just helping to ease housing shortages worldwide; they're also environmentally friendly, foster a sense of community, and add significant property value. Between the global pandemic and extreme weather events driven by the climate crisis, we've all had to grapple with an uncertain future, adapt to new challenges, and embrace sustainable practices. This "new normal" has altered how we live—making us more virtual, mobile, and flexible. These changes have shifted what we need from our homes.

Historically, the concept of "home" has been synonymous with security, tradition, and continuity, but those values don't align with the reality of the new normal. ADUs offer something different: flexibility. And that flexibility is exactly what we need to navigate today's challenges and the uncertainties of tomorrow.

I think of this book as a love letter to ADUs. Back in 2023, I went on an organized ADU tour in Los Angeles. While inside the most beautiful ADU I'd ever seen, gorgeously and painstakingly designed from the ground up by local architecture firm Bunch Design, I kept overhearing people saying, "This is an ADU?" or "I didn't know an ADU could be this nice." I suppose because of their smaller size and relationship to the main house, people assume ADUs won't have architectural beauty or sophisticated design.

I'm excited about the proliferation of ADUs and urban infill architecture as solutions to the global housing crisis. I'm also excited for people to see how fabulous and design forward ADUs can be. I've featured some of the most spectacular, unique, and innovative ADUs I could find in the United States as well as in Canada, Europe, and even Byron Bay, Australia! I hope you find them inspirational during these uncertain and transformative times.

INTRODUCTION

Accessory Dwelling Units (ADUs) are defined by the American Planning Association as "smaller, independent residential dwelling units located on the same lots as stand-alone single-family homes." Like a standard home, an ADU must include all of the spaces and amenities needed for a tenant to live comfortably, including a kitchen, bathroom, living/sleeping spaces, and a completely separate entrance from the main unit. As the name suggests, an ADU is typically smaller than the existing home, ranging anywhere from 500 to 1,000 square feet, although the regulations are changing all the time.

The concept of an ADU isn't new. Throughout history these secondary living spaces have been called in-law units, carriage houses, granny flats, and guest cottages. In Canada, they're called laneway cottages, in New Zealand they are minor dwelling units, and in Sweden it's an enkelrum. For the purposes of this book, we'll call them ADUs. What distinguishes them from small homes and the tiny house movement is that they share the lot with another house. They are, by definition, accessory to a primary residence.

ADUs come in various shapes and sizes, although the most common is a detached, stand-alone unit. These can either be former garages converted into living spaces or newly built structures. ADUs can also be added to the primary residence or carved out of an existing space, like a basement or attic. In certain jurisdictions, if the conversion of space is contained entirely within a single-family residence, it's called a "junior ADU."

ADUs can be constructed using any kind of material or building technique, though local building codes may require certain aesthetic, zoning, or climate-related features.

ADUs are generally built in one of three ways:
Ground-up construction: This refers to building a brand-new ADU that's separate from the primary home. These typically range from 350 to 1,200 square feet and are often located next

to or behind the main house, though the placement can vary. In some cases, homeowners demolish an existing detached garage to replace it with a new structure.

Conversions and additions: This method involves using or expanding existing space to create an ADU. Common options include converting or remodeling a basement, attic, or attached garage. You can also build on top of an attached garage or add an entirely new structure on top of a detached garage. In most areas, the unit must have a separate entrance as well as dedicated amenities such as a bathroom and kitchen to qualify as an ADU.

Prefab: Prefab ADUs are built partially or entirely in a factory and then transported to the site for placement or assembly. There are two main types of prefab ADUs:

→ Manufactured homes, which are constructed entirely off-site.

→ Modular homes, where sections of the ADU are prefabricated off-site and then assembled and finished on-site.

THE ADU LANDSCAPE

As rents continue to soar and entry-level homes in urban areas become scarcer, cities across the US and Canada are embracing ADUs as a critical solution to their housing crises. A 2020 Freddie Mac report revealed a significant rise in the number of US homes with ADUs, growing from just 1 percent to 7 percent over the past two decades. This shift highlights the increasing reliance on ADUs as a means of providing affordable housing options.

States that currently allow ADUs include California, Connecticut, Oregon, Maine, New York, and Washington. A 2021 study by Porch Research estimated that there are around one and a half million ADUs in the US, with over half located in just four states: California (30 percent), Florida (12 percent), Texas (10 percent), and Georgia (5 percent). Los Angeles leads all US cities in ADU construction, reflecting the growing demand for alternative housing solutions in high-density urban areas.

As states and municipalities recognize the many benefits ADUs offer—such as creating affordable housing, generating rental income for homeowners, and increasing housing density without significant urban sprawl—regulations are beginning to relax. Many jurisdictions are reducing permit fees, easing zoning restrictions, and simplifying the approval process to encourage more ADU development. This growing trend signals that ADUs are becoming a key part of the housing landscape, offering a practical solution to meet the evolving needs of homeowners and communities alike.

REGULATIONS

While ADU laws are typically created at the local level, several state legislatures have mandated that cities permit them. Even where ADUs are legal, homeowners must still comply with local zoning codes, which can vary widely within a state. Understanding these local requirements is essential before proceeding with an ADU project.

ADU regulations aim to balance the need for additional housing with preserving the character of existing neighborhoods. Though the permitting process and specific restrictions vary by location, common considerations include:

Building height: Municipalities often impose height restrictions to preserve natural light for neighboring properties. Some jurisdictions base these limits on the width of the lot, while others don't allow ADUs to exceed the height of the primary residence. A typical height limit is 16 feet, though some rooflines may be allowed to slope up to 5 feet higher.

Lili Weigert's earthquake cottage in San Francisco

Building size: Size restrictions vary, with some areas setting minimum and/or maximum size limits. These may be based on the size of the lot or the primary home.

Design: ADUs may need to adhere to design guidelines to ensure architectural compatibility with the primary home or neighborhood.

Setbacks: ADUs are typically required to be set back a certain distance from side and rear property lines, with common setbacks being 4 or 5 feet.

Parking: While some jurisdictions require one off-street parking space for an ADU, many are removing this requirement.

Occupancy and ownership: In many areas, ADUs cannot be owned separately from the primary residence. Some jurisdictions also require the homeowner to live on-site for the ADU to be rented.

FINANCING

There's a reason loan officer Meredith Munger advises homeowners to find an expert with ADU-financing experience: It's complicated! In the mortgage industry, historically ADUs haven't been considered rentable space. The term "ADU" has typically referred to a pool house, shed, or granny flat—not a rented space. So, government finance agencies aren't sure how to treat ADUs, because they lack historical data to show the long-term value they add to a property. This can be a challenge for traditional lenders. "It's a bit of a chicken-and-egg problem," Munger says. "There's not enough data for lenders to figure out how to underwrite the projects, but without the loans there's no way to generate more data."

Munger, who is one of the largest ADU-focused lenders in California, is confident that things will get easier. According to the state of California, more than 45,000 ADUs were initiated in 2023, while new home construction dropped below 60,000. Munger believes that 2024 will be the first year we see ADU construction outpace new home construction. "These projects are becoming a national phenomenon as more communities grapple with shortages of affordable housing and the need to increase density," she says.

MEREDITH MUNGER'S ADVICE

FIGURE OUT HOW YOU'RE GOING TO PAY FOR YOUR ADU UP FRONT.

ADUs are financed as part of the existing property (i.e., a first or second mortgage). If there isn't enough equity for a cash-out refinance or a home equity line of credit (HELOC), you can look into construction and renovation loans. These are based on the value after the ADU is completed. You'll need to talk to a bank that specializes in these types of loans. (A bank that doesn't do construction and renovation loans will say you don't qualify because you don't have enough equity.)

GET PREAPPROVED BEFORE YOU SPEND A DIME.

Even if you don't do the loan until closer to construction, get preapproved so you know your budget. Every loan is individual, and often it's based on your personal income and not potential rental income. I see too many clients spend $50,000 on designs and permits for a champagne castle only to find out that they're on a beer budget. Also, mortgage guidelines sometimes dictate what you can build, so it's important you understand those before you start designing and submitting permits. Fannie Mae, for example, will only allow you to build one ADU. However, there are work-arounds. You can include unlimited "room additions," or permit a second ADU as an office and plumb for a future kitchen. Once the unit is built, it can be rezoned as an ADU.

CALCULATE YOUR ROI (RETURN ON INVESTMENT) BASED ON YOUR LONG-TERM PLANS AND FINANCIAL GOALS.

If you do this right, you can finance 100 percent of the cost of construction with no down payment and no out-of-pocket costs. Even if you plan to have family members live in the ADU, you need a long-term backup plan. If you build a two-bedroom for your parents, could you then divide it in half and have two one-bedrooms to rent? In that case, you'd want to design it with two bathrooms. Most people think that building a three-bedroom ADU to rent will optimize their ROI but what it actually does is optimize the number of kids destroying your backyard and banging up the property. If you intend to rent, we generally find that one-bedrooms are the optimal ROI. So, if you have space for a three-bedroom house, consider building three one-bedroom units to optimize your rental income.

Conversely, if you intend to sell off the unit, then building a three-bedroom ADU is often your best ROI because it will sell for more than a combination of three one-bedroom ADUs. Generally speaking, with the exception of garage conversions, I find that selling off the unit has a better return on investment over ten years than renting it out.

DON'T GO FOR THE LOWEST BID, GO FOR THE "ALL IN" BID.

Construction bids should be within $5,000 to $10,000 of each other. Bids are based on the cost of materials plus the cost of labor, and those are usually dollar for dollar equal. The general contractor typically adds 15 to 20 percent, which is standard.

Construction bid =
(materials cost + labor cost) +
15% profit margin

If you see a bid that's lowballing the others, that's somebody who doesn't know what they're doing.

As a banker, my occupational hazard is bad contractors, so I advise my clients to do their due diligence before signing any contracts:

Make sure they have a contractor's license, insurance, and worker's compensation.

Check references, reviews, and lines of credit.

Search litigation involving the company and the individuals in the company, including their past construction work with other companies. Many contractors have had some litigation in the past; the question is, how serious was it? If it was a minor dispute over a few leftover sheets of plywood, don't worry about it, but if it involved serious construction defects, run like the wind.

DON'T FREAK OUT ABOUT CONSTRUCTION COSTS. FOCUS ON THE MONTHLY PAYMENT INSTEAD!

Generally speaking, every $100,000 you spend on construction will cost approximately $600 per month. If you spend $300,000 on your ADU, your monthly payment will be $1,800. Where can you rent a house for $1,800 a month? Or buy one for $300,000? That's when you realize ADUs are a great deal.

MEREDITH MUNGER'S FIVE FAQs

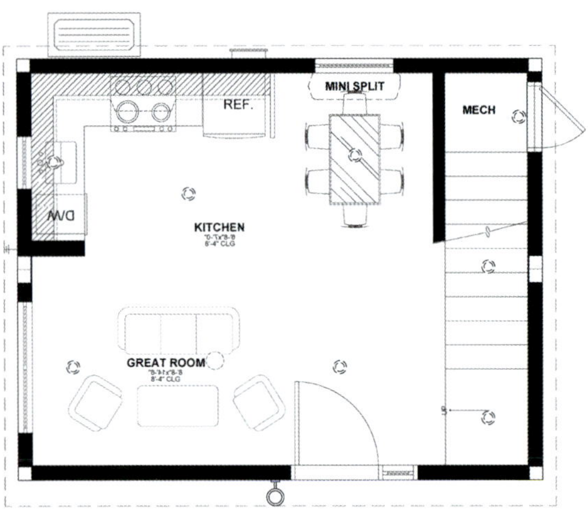

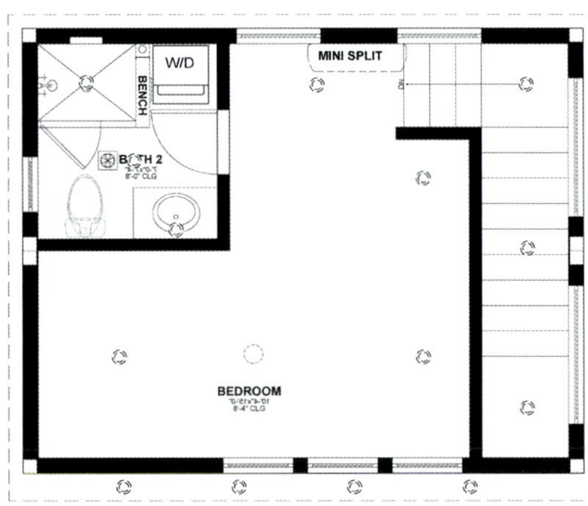

top
Asymmetrical roof lines are approximately 50 percent of the cost of triangular roof lines.

bottom
Plumbing aligned along one wall is called a "wet wall."

1. ARE THERE SEPARATE LOANS FOR ADUS?

No. ADUs are always financed as part of the real estate.

2. WILL AN ADU INCREASE MY PROPERTY TAXES?

The assessor looks at the cost to build the ADU and multiplies that by 1 percent. So, if you submit permits for a $120,000 build, that's $1,200 per year/$100 per month. I typically see a monthly increase of between $100 and $150.

3. IF I BUILD AN ADU ON MY PARENTS' PROPERTY, CAN I GET A SEPARATE LOAN?

More likely you'd both apply for the loan, and we'd title it as "joint tenants." You'd own the ADU and be responsible for the loan payments, and your parents would own the primary house and the land.

Follow up: If I own the ADU, how do I keep the inheritance of the property fair for my other siblings?

Either by selling off the ADU to you or by titling the ADU as "joint tenants." That allows your parents to bequeath the house and the land equally among siblings or as they see fit.

4. HOW CAN I REDUCE CONSTRUCTION COSTS?

Be honest with your architect and general contractor about your budget and discuss "value engineering" the project. There are many ways to bring costs down without impacting the beauty and luxury of the ADU.

Consider pouring sleek cement floors with epoxy, eliminating $20,000 in floor tile cost.

Keep your rooflines simple. Asymmetrical rooflines are approximately 50 percent of the cost of triangular rooflines.

Align all plumbing into one wall—we call it a "wet wall"—and face the plumbing and utilities to the area closest to the utility connection. That way you don't need to trench or add utilities all around the house, which saves quite a bit of cost.

5. SHOULD I DIY MY ADU?

I don't encourage it. DIYers often end up taking far longer and costing themselves more than proficient contractors who have the process streamlined.

ADU STORIES

Mar Vista, California

ARCHITECT

Oonagh Ryan, ORA

LIL' RED

Lil' Red was part of a new build in Mar Vista, a family-oriented neighborhood on the Westside of Los Angeles. In 2014, a young couple bought the 6,650-square-foot plot after running out of space in nearby Venice Beach. They wanted a new home plus an ADU they'd use as an art studio.

"Since we developed the project on a cleared site, we were able to use the space in a more creative way," says architect Oonagh Ryan. Instead of building to the edge of the lot lines, which is common for new developments in the area, Ryan set the structures back and buffered them with outdoor spaces. "We positioned the home and the ADU to take full advantage of indoor/outdoor living," Ryan says. "We also fit a carport and a 45-foot lap pool."

While the main house and the ADU have their own characteristics, they playfully complement one another. The house, a white two-story bar, is shaped like a boomerang. The shape allows for expanded views through the house to the gardens beyond. The ADU is a bright red studio shaped like a Chinese take-out box. Its peaked roof matches the single-story gable cottages that are prevalent in the neighborhood.

Because Lil' Red would initially function as an art studio, Ryan positioned the vaulted skylight at the optimal angle to capture even northern light throughout the year. She included large doors on two sides to accommodate art projects and make it easy to move materials through the studio. The doors also connect the indoor space to the courtyards on either side of the building.

Considering that the family's needs will evolve and change over time, Lil' Red also needed to be multifunctional. It's equipped with everything it needs to function as an independent living space and, although at only 291 square feet its footprint is small, the vaulted ceilings and abundant access to the outdoors make it feel much larger.

For now, Lil' Red is serving as an art studio, a pool cabana, and an extra play space. It turns out that it's also a great party room. When the family hosts gatherings, guests use Lil' Red like a passageway connecting the front of the property to the pool and back gardens. Often they'll stop, pausing to appreciate the unique and special space.

Wide doors on both sides of the ADU allow for maximum flow and access between the entry courtyard at the front of the property and the backyard patio area and pool.

right and below
Designed with flexibility in mind, the ADU is attached to the house and accessible directly from the entry foyer. The door can be left open for a direct connection to the house or sealed off so the ADU can function as a separate, independent unit.

opposite
Inspired by visionary artist James Turrell's Skyspaces, a north-facing skylight infuses the space with natural light. As a focal point, it's positioned to project the interplay between the ever-shifting patterns of light and shadow within the unique architectural form.

above
Fully equipped to function as a living space, the ADU is currently used as an art studio.

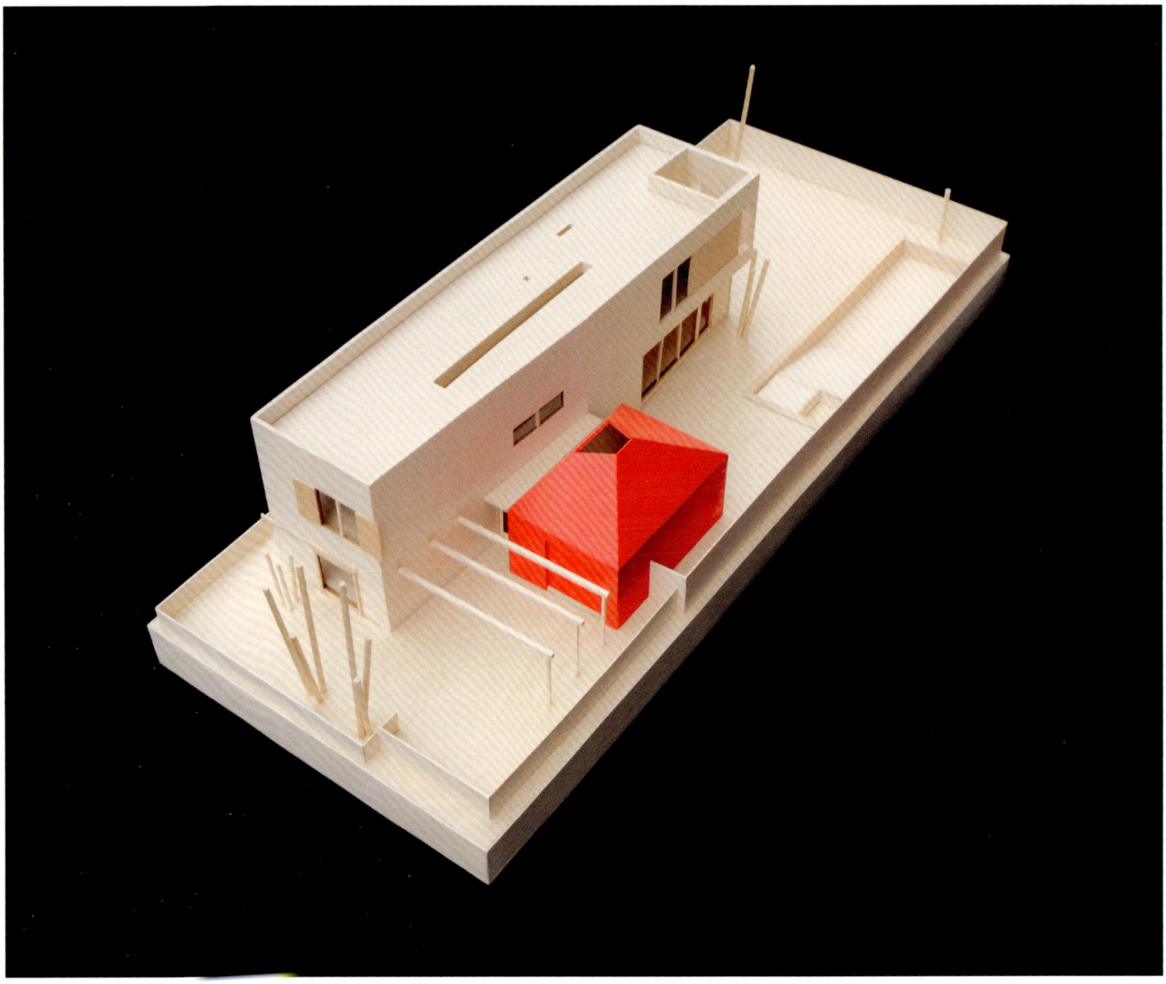

Deprioritizing on-site parking and creating two independent structures allows for a variety of flexible outdoor spaces that connect the house to the ADU.

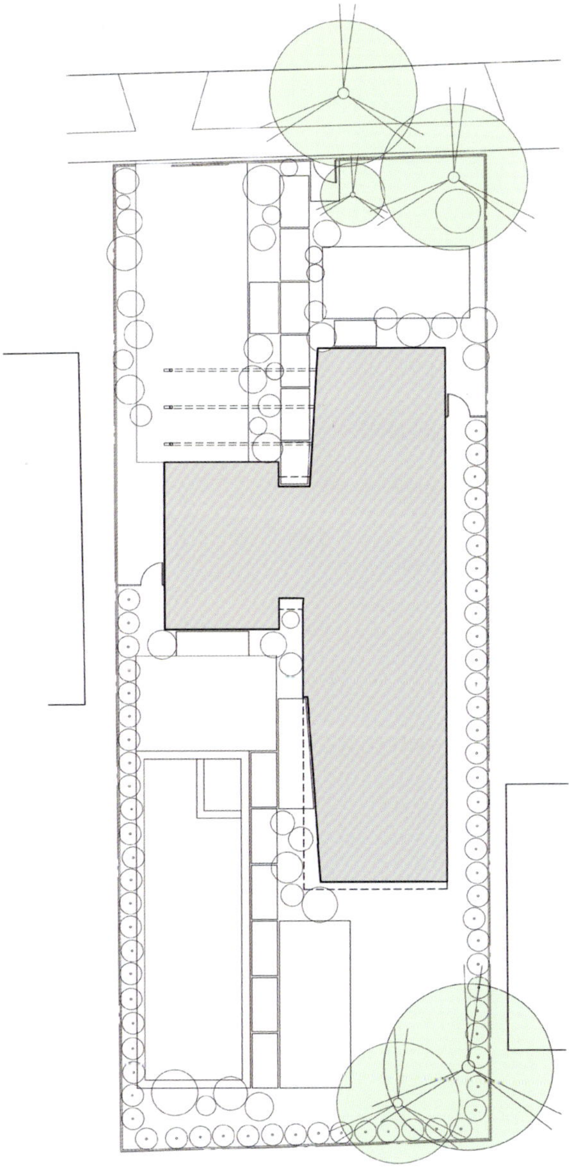

above
The color, Dunn-Edwards's Red Ink, was inspired by a strawberry bush at the owner's former home.

left
Architectural rendering shows setbacks on all sides to include outdoor spaces and create a sense of privacy for the property.

GARDEN STUDIO

Byron Bay, Australia

ARCHITECT
Harley Graham (HGA Studio)

In 2017, Byron Bay–based architect Harley Graham of HGA Studio designed this 485-square-foot ADU for television personality Shelley Craft. A well-known figure in the Australian real estate world, Craft hosts a popular reality series called *The Block*, which follows four or five couples as they renovate houses and compete to sell them for the highest price at auction.

Craft asked Graham to build a multipurpose space in her back garden. She wanted an extra living area/outdoor refuge that could also serve as a separate guesthouse for visiting friends and family.

"She has a real penchant for mid-century modern design," Graham says about Craft, whose primary house was designed by noted Australian modern architect Paul Uhlmann. "We wanted to respect the modern aesthetic by adding an ADU

top
The 485-square-foot ADU is wrapped in tallowwood and constructed on a floating concrete slab.

bottom
Architectural renderings show the ADU from above and from street level.

The modern roofline over a small pool cabana echoes the ADU's, connecting the architectural elements in the backyard.

with 'mid-century flair.'" The ADU's clean lines and warm, open spaces complement the primary house while celebrating the unique features of the self-contained dwelling.

Mid-century modern is a style that Graham is very comfortable with. "We look at a lot of mid-century design because it's so climate responsive," he says. Built with locally sourced tallowwood and constructed on a floating concrete slab, the studio was designed to make the most of the subtropical climate. Cross ventilation and strategically positioned awnings regulate the temperature all year around. "You can open up the entire building and it works, whether it's in tropical rains or harsh sun," Graham says.

Glass walls and clerestory windows flood the ADU with light. The interior design and furnishings are minimal yet cheerful, including select pieces from the homeowner's art collection.

5864

MODERN CRAFTSMAN

Hollywood, California

ARCHITECT
Bunch Design

In 2023, architects Hisako Ichiki and Bo Sundius of Bunch Design replaced an old garage with this craftsman-style home, stacking a 400-square-foot office over a 950-square-foot ADU. "They wanted a place for their parents to live for part of the year and they also wanted a separate home office so they could get work done," Sundius says of his clients, an author and a video game developer. "It was the perfect post-pandemic script."

Located in the heart of Hollywood, the property is next to a procession of original craftsman homes that lead to historic Hollywood and the Hollywood sign. Built on a corner lot, the building fronts a public street, something the team considered when deciding on height, proportions, colors, and material. "We wanted the building to integrate within the existing context of the neighborhood while introducing a fresh modern presence to the street," Ichiki says.

Constructed mostly of Siberian larch and dyed wood shingles, the building fits nicely into the block. It's an active and social street, close to bars and restaurants, where neighbors walk their dogs. On the second floor, a natural larch wood balcony perches over the street like a stage, screened in by vertical lattice. The shingle wall on the balcony screens the office from the street. A rain planter full of succulents serves as a partition between the front of the building and the sidewalk.

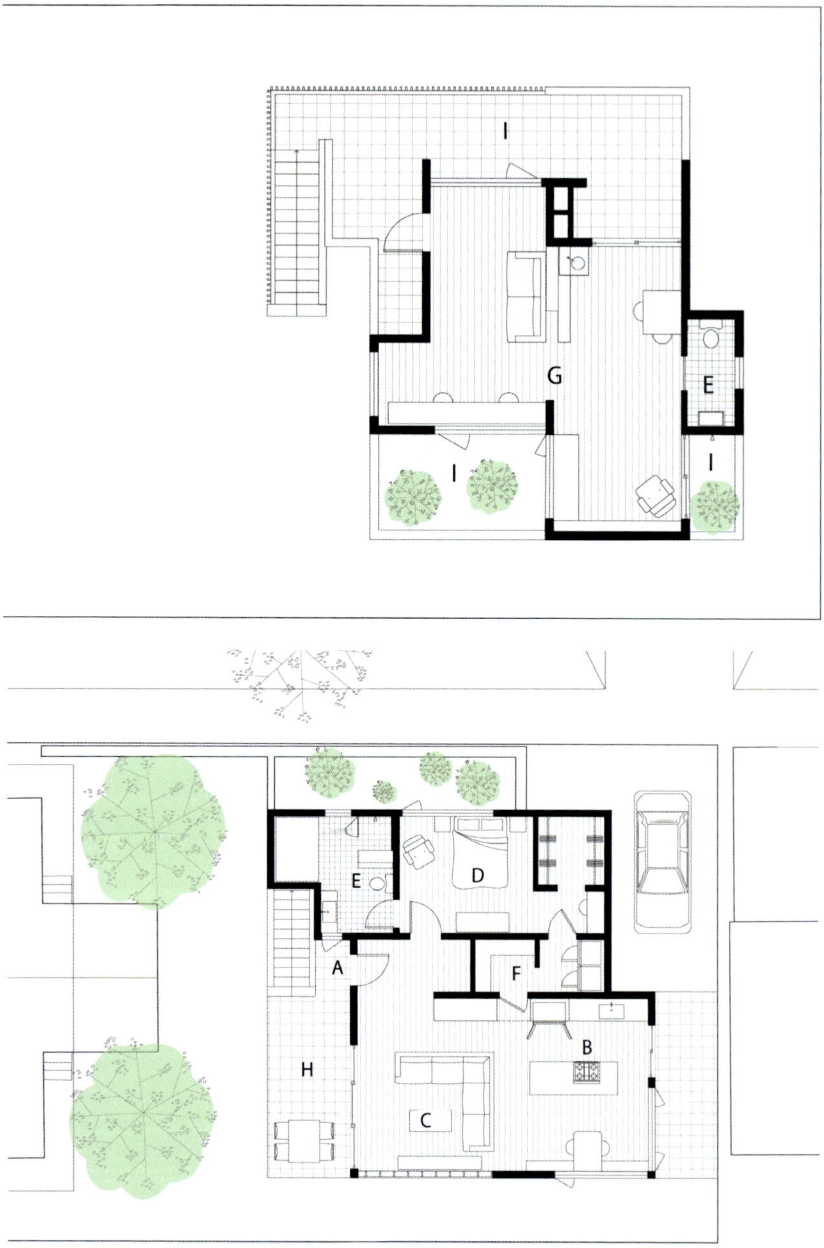

Diagrams show how the spaces on both levels are organized.

A. entry
B. kitchen/ dining
C. living room
D. bedroom
E. bathroom
F. laundry/ pantry
G. office
H. patio
I. balcony

top
The kitchen on the lower level opens up to the back of the property, where the neighbor's white garage wall reflects light back into the room. Simple wood built-ins organize the space and reduce visual clutter.

bottom
The ceiling pops up to create volume in the living room while also creating space for a garden in the office above.

opposite
A full bath and sauna are tucked under the stairwell of the exterior stairs that connect the ADU to the office above.

above
An outdoor shower is tucked into the corner of the deck off the library.

The upper level includes space for a large office and an adjacent library.

The sunny library opens onto an
80-square-foot private patio.

GUEST PAVILION

Catalonia, Spain

ARCHITECT
NordEst Arquitectura

As part of their practice, architects Miquel Rusca and Jordi Riembau of NordEst Arquitectura investigate how a place can keep surprises. With the Guest Pavilion, a 900-square-foot glass box perched over Spain's northeastern coast, it comes naturally.

Designed in 2014 for a family from Switzerland, the Guest Pavilion is in the popular fishing village of Begur, known for its spectacular stretch of the Costa Brava coastline. The primary house, built in 2000, was part of a mini-development of two houses similar in size and design. After spending some time at the house, the family fell in love with the region and its natural beauty. "They're in the middle of nature," Rusca says. "There's nothing in front of them except the sea and a forested hill that's protected so nobody else can build there."

The Guest Pavilion was built to accommodate guests when the main house is full. This happens every summer, Riembau explains, as the main house only has three bedrooms, and the family has many guests. "They liked the idea of integrating a structure into this piece of forest that was totally separate," Rusca says. "We never talked about it, but I suppose they also wanted to put their own stamp on something. The main house was completely done when they bought it."

Located 50 feet south of the main house, the first surprise the Guest Pavilion keeps is the view. "We thought a lot about how we could access the structure while keeping the views to our backs," Rusca says. They considered building a high path that cut back and accessed the structure from above, but instead they decided to place the entrance in front, where the basement level was carved into the steep, rocky slope. "You have to go into the land before you can access the rest," Riembau says. Once inside, you discover the views when you reach the main level: the sea on one side and the dense forest in front. "It feels like a floating treehouse," he says.

"What we had in mind was a very thin and light box floating on the forest," Rusca says. "We didn't want to be the protagonist or change the feeling by destroying or removing anything. We're very sensitive to the landscape integration."

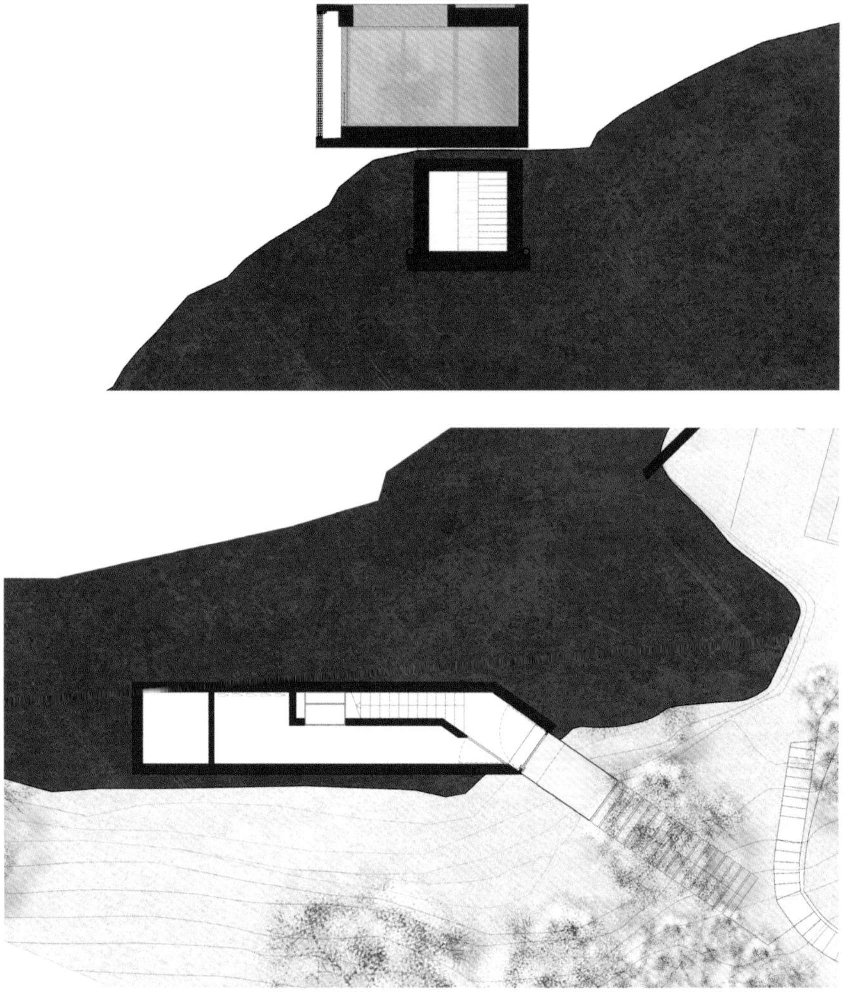

Architectural renderings depict how the structure's foundation allows the upper level to "float" over the steep hillside.

The entrance to the ADU is through the basement, which is built into the land and also serves as the foundation for the house.

Integrating the ADU into the natural landscape was a priority for the architects. "We don't want to become the protagonist, we want to be part of it," Miquel Rusca says.

A rectangle of glass, the structure is encased by electronically powered steel slats. "You can close everything up to create a totally closed box or open it all up to feel part of the forest," Riembau says. The main level is an open space with a small kitchen that appears or disappears, also controlled by an electronic system. The closet and bathroom run along the northern side, which is also the coldest side. "It's very simple but it has lots of details," Rusca says. "A lot of thought went into a lot of small things."

Another surprise is a secret door, just inside the entrance. "We did a very nice integration here," says Rusca. "Everything is concrete but the door is wood. We matched it." Through the camouflaged door, a hallway leads to a tiny mechanical room. In the bonus space in between, the architects surprised the homeowners with a custom wine cellar.

"It wasn't in the plan," Rusca says, explaining how they'd needed more anchorage than expected to support the half of the structure cantilevered over the forest. "This basement fixes the structure to the land," he says. "This whole level was meant to be used as a foundation."

The wine cellar is clean and spare. Steel brackets support the bottles so all you see is the wine. "We were playing with minimal materials and color," Riembau says. "In this space, the protagonist is the wine." Was the homeowner surprised? "He couldn't stop laughing," Riembau says. "He told us we'd solved one of his problems because he didn't have a wine cellar in his house."

left
The wine room on the ground level.

below left
The staircase leading up to the first floor.

below right
A wooden door off the entrance is camouflaged, treated and painted to match the concrete.

A remote-controlled system of slats can open the space completely to connect with the surroundings or close everything up into a tight box.

The main level consists of a simple, open space.

A small kitchen appears and disappears, operated by a remote electronic charger.

THE CURVE

Woodland Hills, California

ARCHITECT
Navid Masoudi (MASS Architecture & Design Group)

INTERIOR DESIGN
Azadeh Garshasbi (Blend Studio)

The Curve is the first collaboration between architect Navid Masoudi and interior designer Azadeh Garshasbi. Designed for a family in suburban Los Angeles who plan to use it for rental income, the 1,100-square-foot ADU is a modern open space with a two-bedroom loft.

Because the 1964 five-bedroom home is located on a cul-de-sac, the offset from the road is crescent-shaped. That meant that while the lot itself is relatively large (almost a third of an acre), the shape forced the team to think outside of the typical cubist form. To find the space they needed, they added a second floor to the existing attached garage, connecting that to the rest of the ADU via an internal staircase. The smooth white stucco facade along the front mimics the gentle curve of the offset.

Constructing a curved wall can be quite involved, but this curve was gentle enough to make structural integrity and load distribution issues less complicated. More challenging was adding the tall, narrow windows. Installing a window on a curved wall is an exercise in precision, from measuring to cutting and fitting to ensuring proper sealing and insulation. Strategically placed along the curved wall, the five linear windows accentuate the elegant curve and bring in natural light and dynamic light patterns.

Although The Curve is entirely self-contained—with its own entrance, parking spot, and private outdoor space—the goal was for the new structure to blend seamlessly into the old, resulting in a cohesive architectural ensemble. To connect the new element, the team chose a palette of finishes, accents, and colors that creates a natural flow between the ADU, garage, and main residence.

Photographic renderings depict The Curve as a cohesive and elegant addition to the existing property.

opposite
Known for his sleek and modern design, architect Navid Masoudi has received many awards for his work in his hometown of Shiraz, Iran. One of his trademarks is incorporating one red feature into each project—in this case, the exposed beam in the kitchen.

right
Inspired by the principles of modern minimalism and Scandinavian design, designer Azadeh Garshasbi chose an all-white palette and simple wood finishes that honor the clean lines, open space, and natural light of the structure.

below
The focal point of the interior is the striking wooden staircase, a bold architectural statement that ascends from the kitchen to the second level.

SPACE: MAXIMIZING PERCEPTIONS AND EXPERIENCES

"The plan proceeds from within to without; the exterior is the result of the interior."

—LE CORBUSIER

Hisako Ichiki and Bo Sundius think a lot about space. As cofounders of Los Angeles–based Bunch Design, the architects are committed to adding housing and density to the famously sprawling and congested city.

With an estimated one and three-quarter million additional residents expected to arrive in Los Angeles County by 2030, Ichiki and Sundius believe that ADUs are a sustainable antidote to the impending housing crisis. "We believe in ADUs because we believe in Los Angeles," Sundius says. "By adding housing to homeowners' backyards, we're building within the existing infrastructure and adding flexibility to the single-family home."

Ichiki and Sundius have already designed more than thirty ADUs, ranging in size from 300 to 1,200 square feet. Generally located behind a primary residence, their location and small footprint challenge the architects to reconsider and prioritize what people need most from their living spaces. "Residential architecture has been more about curb appeal and front lawns," Sundius says. "Even though we spend 90 percent of our time inside these buildings, the space we inhabit is often a secondary thought."

Ichiki and Sundius design ADUs from the inside out, considering the volume first; how the design appears from the outside is a result of interior decisions. "We think about adjacencies, and how the client may live in the space over time," Sundius says. "We shape the volume with windows, height, color, and light to create a changing and delightful interior environment that fits loosely around the inhabitant."

While each ADU is unique, the pair has developed a set of guidelines that they weave into each project. Inspired by an "inside-out" design approach, they draw from Japanese spatial strategies, an interest in the use of everyday spaces, and a critique of outdated developer-driven residential space design. "If you do these things, you'll have a spatially focused design strategy," says Ichiki.

"Just as you perceive space, you can also alter perception."

—BO SUNDIUS

"We scan the horizon to establish what is possible, just as we map edges and corners to find limits and enclosure."

—BO SUNDIUS

BO SUNDIUS: ON SPACE

When you walk into a room, you immediately look to the edges. You notice the corners—where the walls meet walls, where the walls meet the floor and ceiling. You subconsciously clock the corners and assess the boundaries of your space.

But the space I just described could also describe a box, and we humans typically don't like getting boxed in. As we become subconsciously aware of the edges, we form opinions and feelings related to those boundaries. We have questions: "Is the space large enough?" "Can I move around freely?" "What is the path of escape, physically or even mindfully?" If a space is dark or low-ceilinged, you may feel anxious or wary. If a space has light-filled corners, you may feel more relaxed and buoyant.

By understanding how space is perceived, you can design a space to be perceived in different ways. If you want to make a small space feel large, you can design for that. You could call it the "illusionist architect," where the designer crafts a series of moves, using sleight of hand if necessary, actively trying to shape spatial perception to their desired goal.

WELCOME HOME

No matter where it's located on the property, an ADU deserves the features that identify it as a home.

"If you give an ADU all the dignified characteristics of the front house—its own entryway, a nice front door, a light next to the doorknob—it feels like you're arriving at an actual home and not a backyard afterthought."

—BO SUNDIUS

EXPANDED BOUNDARY

Interiors feel larger when they're connected to outdoor spaces. Prioritize accessible outdoor spaces whenever possible.

"Even if you're close to the property line you can still make a big opening. If a window looks right at a wall, just put up some 'growies' or plant something there."

—BO SUNDIUS

"We'll pull the building farther from the property line than we're required. If the minimum is four feet, we'll go up to ten. Four feet is completely useless, but when you pull back six more, you actually have a miniature backyard."

—HISAKO ICHIKI

BORROWED VIEW

Views that are farther away and more expansive give a sense of largesse to the space.

"We put clerestory windows wherever we can. It makes the ceiling feel like it's floating, and all you see are mountains or the sky."

—BO SUNDIUS

"If you're in a 500-square-foot house, your frame of reference is probably less than 10 feet away. But when you have a window with a distant view of a mountain, the physical act of your eyeball recalibrating to focus on something far away triggers a sense of space."

—HISAKO ICHIKI

NEW SKY

Vault the ceiling. By lifting the ceiling, it gives you a sense of height and you can see farther.

"Interior walls can do what they need to functionally without going to the ceiling. If you bring them all the way up, they start to block the expanded ceiling."
—HISAKO ICHIKI

“Lifting the ceiling is one of the ways we try to blur where the walls meet the ceiling because that intersection feels like the end of the space.”

—BO SUNDIUS

RELEASE SPACE

This is a Japanese concept related to internal spatial organization and sequencing, opening and connecting spaces.

"Repetition of shapes or structural elements can make a space feel larger by emphasizing the feeling of continued space. "We use repetition as a tactic. By repeating the triangle divider, you see it almost elongated."

—BO SUNDIUS

"Anytime you see something repeat itself, it makes it feel bigger. You get a forced perspective."

—HISAKO ICHIKI

PASSAGE ISLAND

Vancouver, British Columbia

BUILDER
Honomobo

Passage Island is a quaint little island of thirty-five homes off the coast of Vancouver. There's no ferry service, but you can get to downtown Vancouver in twenty minutes by boat. In 2021, a couple who owned an older home on the island decided to build an ADU. "Their kids were getting older and they wanted their own space," says Daniel Engelman, founder of Edmonton-based Honomobo modular homes. "They were looking for a respite."

The homeowners chose one of Honomobo's 640-square-foot models after realizing how expensive and time-consuming it would be to build on-site. "We can do it a lot faster," says Engelman. "With us, it's just, here's the set and here's the cost."

The couple, avid sailors who are based in Vancouver, wanted the ADU to provide abundant indoor/outdoor living spaces and to take advantage of the surrounding ocean views. "If you want a lot of glass, our homes make a lot of sense," Engelman says. This model has an engineered steel frame and weatherproof Cor-Ten steel siding to support multiple walls of floor-to-ceiling windows and sliding doors. "It's a beautiful, modern space," he says. "They love it."

above
Roughly 90 percent of the one-bedroom, one-bath ADU was completed in a factory, then shipped to the property via barge.

right
"There's only one company in Vancouver that has a crane mounted on the barge, so we went with them. They had to measure the length of the lift versus the weight of the modules to make sure we could do it. When it came time to lift, we had to go through tide charts and make sure the water level was at the right height. It was quite a thing."
—Daniel Engelman

Perched over the rocky slope, the
640-square-foot ADU is surrounded
by decks and sweeping, unobstructed
ocean views.

The simple, modern interior was designed to maximize the views. Glass walls and sliding panels seamlessly connect the indoor and outdoor spaces.

ALLEY CAT

Minneapolis, Minnesota

ARCHITECT
Christopher Strom (CSA)

Architect Christopher Strom believes that the ADUs he designs throughout urban Minneapolis are "a net gain," creating much-needed housing, limiting the carbon footprint by fitting into the existing grid and urban infrastructure, and adding value for homeowners. "They're a way to turbocharge your property without wrecking what was there before," he says.

In 2019, Strom designed Alley Cat for a couple who wanted to rent out their primary house and move into a new space. The 554-square-foot one-bedroom ADU is over a two-car garage, which is the most common configuration he builds. "It's a cultural aspiration to have an indoor garage in Minnesota," he says. "You don't want to scrape your windows and shovel out your car all winter."

The structure is all new construction, which is typical because most garages don't have the structural design called "frost footings" required in cold climates to prevent frost heaves from damaging a building's structural integrity. Instead, most garages are built on floating slabs that allow them to move with the ground as it freezes and thaws, but they don't work under the additional weight of a residential space. "People ask about building over an existing garage all the

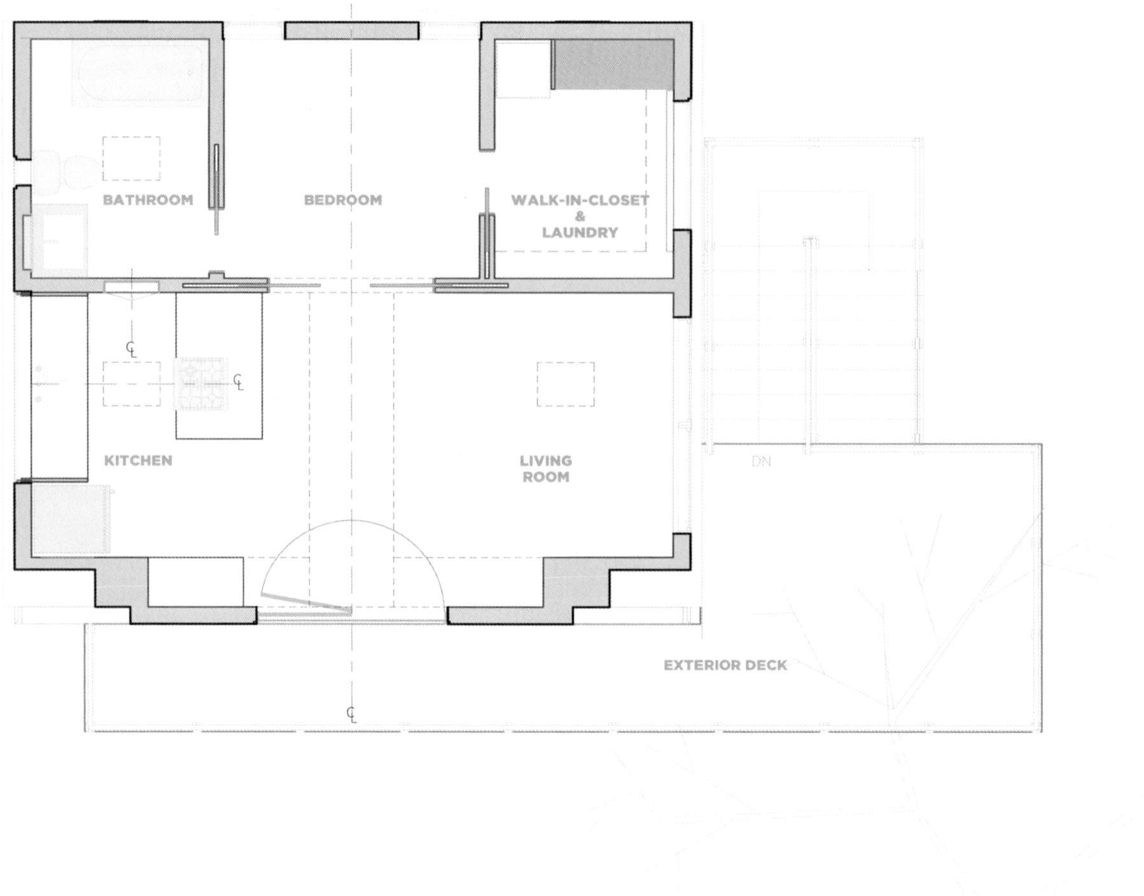

Design plan shows how the new structure shares the space with an existing tree in the backyard.

time," Strom says. "But we've only done it once, because the garage had footings."

Alley Cat is accessed from an alley, eliminating the need for a driveway cutting through the property and taking up space. And on this property, space is important because the ADU shares the backyard with an immense catalpa tree. "As far as we know, it might be the biggest catalpa in the state," Strom says. "It's freakishly huge." Strom placed the structure as far from the tree as possible. "We didn't want to threaten the roots," he says.

As an added challenge, the homeowners had their hearts set on a gable roof, which can be difficult to incorporate with ADU height restrictions. "Gables are cute, but you lose a lot of square footage when you bring the roof down to the floor," Strom says. To make it work for the couple—who are both quite tall—Strom added continuous shed dormers to gain usable living space behind the pointed profile of the gable.

Warm-toned butcher block is used throughout the kitchen for work surfaces and for a portal around the window to showcase the view. The custom-designed "cat house" has a motion light that's activated by a cat-sized flapping door.

Outside and inside view of the same corner. The gabled roof is demarcated by custom shelving and a built-in cabinet that hugs the sloped ceiling.

Double pocket doors separate the bedroom from the living room. "Pocketed doors save space and allow us to make the bedroom relatively compact," Strom says. "Most of our clients keep these doors open even when they're sleeping." A skylight and a tall, thin window bring natural light into the en suite bathroom.

Sausalito, California

DESIGN

Loring Sagan and Periscope Homes

CLOUDVIEW

When acclaimed Bay Area designer Loring Sagan first tried to build an ADU behind his Sausalito property in 2014, he was denied. "I applied for a permit to replace an old garden shed with a small cottage/bathroom but the town wouldn't let us," he says. "They said the site was too small."

When California passed pro-ADU legislation in 2018, Sagan became an advisor for a start-up called Periscope Homes. "It was a group of designers and engineers from Tesla and Apple who believed technology could expedite the assembly of buildings," Sagan says. "The vision was to build houses from a kit of parts, like cars." Combining his experience in architecture and design with their knowledge of software and manufacturing, Sagan and Periscope designed their first prototype: a 380-square-foot ADU for Sagan's hillside terrace.

It's hard to imagine a more difficult building site than the top of Sausalito, where narrow, winding roads crisscross and houses perch dramatically over steep hills. "It was the perfect prototype," Sagan says. "Solve for the most difficult obstacles up front, and the rest will be easy." From the parking area, the site is multiple flights of more than eighty steps down, following a meandering path that zigzags past two other houses and a vegetable garden before skirting Sagan's own house. "You couldn't get a crane down there," Sagan says. "You can only use handheld equipment."

To build a foundation on such a challenging site, the team set up a large generator in the parking area that powered a portable hydraulic drilling rig. Unstable soil conditions required drilling six 25-foot-deep pilings to bedrock with an 18-inch auger drill. Then a pump truck poured concrete into the engineered foundation from above. Digging, drilling, and pouring concrete took five weeks. "We built a rock-solid frame in a seismic zone on the side of a hill that's impossible to get to," Sagan says.

The rest of the structure—delivered in parts by flatbed trucks and assembled on-site—is "a matter of aesthetics," says Sagan. The town required that the outside of the ADU match the cedar-shingled main house, but the inside was inspired by a Japanese temple. "I grew up in Japan where there's a 'less is more' aesthetic," he says. "It's about the quality of the materials and the space." The warm and light-filled studio, with sweeping views of the San Francisco Bay, is an exercise in what Sagan calls "elemental design." "There's no trim or decorations," he says. "The structure is the beauty of it."

The concrete foundation was poured from a pump truck in the parking area above the main house. The rest of the structure was delivered in parts and assembled on-site.

top
Panels were brought in on flatbed trucks in specific sequences.

bottom
The old garden shed had running water but no bathroom.

above and left
The designer/homeowner and his wife use the ADU every day, either for working out or as a guesthouse for friends and family.

opposite top
The living roof was delivered in interlocking pallets of pregrown sedum. It mitigates the unit's visual presence from above, and the soil adds an additional layer of insulation. LED lighting illuminates the warm cedar ceiling from behind a valance, and LED strip lighting is recessed into the structural trusses. "The idea was to not have any visible light fixtures," says Sagan.

opposite bottom
From the top of Sausalito, the ADU has sweeping views over the bay with the city of San Francisco in the distance.

GARAGE MAHAL

ARCHITECT
Ileana Schinder

Argentinian architect Ileana Schinder has designed more than forty ADUs throughout Washington, DC, building from the ground up or converting existing spaces into livable units. About a third of her projects are garage makeovers, a popular choice in DC because of the ubiquitous service alleys that allow for direct rear access. Converting an existing structure is also an easier project for a homeowner to take on: "You're more likely to do it if there's already something there," Schinder says. "You don't need to go through the mental process of picturing a structure that doesn't exist."

Why did you start designing ADUs?
In 2016, DC passed a new residential zoning law allowing two units per property, so you could legally renovate a garage or basement and convert it into a new dwelling. The idea evolved almost naturally, out of a need to find space for more housing and the new laws allowing us to do it. ADUs are very popular now in DC as income generators and because they're so easy to implement within the existing housing stock.

Why are ADUs important in Washington?
The cost of housing here is very high and there aren't enough single-family homes for everyone who might want one. Also, households are significantly smaller than they used to be in the 1910s or 1920s when many of these houses were built, so we have lots of housing stock that's not properly sized. Instead of families of six or eight, families of three—or just a couple with a dog—are standard now in urban environments.

Why garages?
Nowadays, having a covered garage in an urban environment isn't an asset, especially if it can be converted into a money generator. You devalue the space if you have a car in there! Modern cars are designed so there's no mechanical need for them to be covered, and the old garages here are too small for current cars anyway. Also, you can still carve out a designated spot for parking somewhere else on your property.

What's next?
I see more jurisdictions allowing for duplexes and triplexes to be built on properties that were previously only zoned for single-family homes. It could exponentially increase our housing stock. I also think they'll reconsider the mandatory owner occupancy laws. DC is such a transient city, and there's no reason why a homeowner needs to be there instead of a tenant.

BRIGHTWOOD 2022

This ADU is used for guests and as a rental unit. It includes a play area and outdoor parking with a car charger. "We try to introduce infrastructure that's a little more geared for the future," Schinder says. "You might not have an electric car today, but chances are you will in ten years."

Schinder transformed this unused garage into a fully functioning studio home with a separate entrance and dedicated parking space.

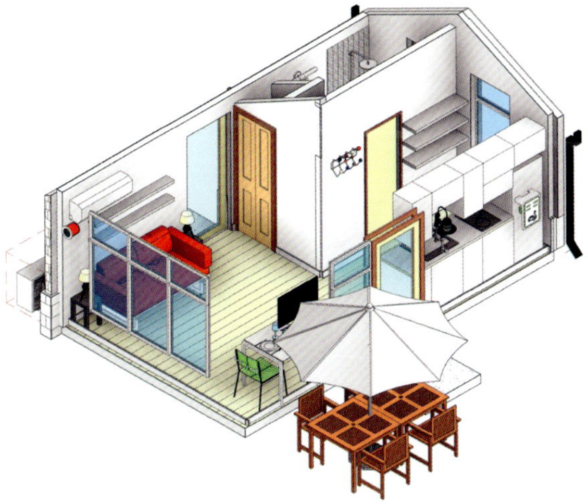

16TH STREET HEIGHTS 2018

Schinder's first ADU set the parameters for future projects in terms of zoning, building, time management, finishes, and equipment. "We realized it wasn't about pushing things to be smaller, but to be 'ADU perfect,'" she says. "We cemented a lot of ideas and became a lot more efficient."

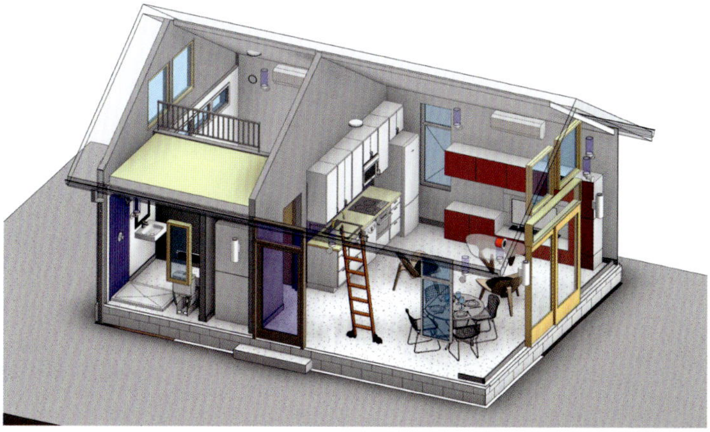

This 1950s garage was transformed into a one-bedroom, one-bathroom ADU with an open kitchen and living space. The exterior preserves the original cedar shake siding, which the architect painted an eye-catching bright blue.

TAKOMA PARK 2020

Schinder's client wanted a flexible space, so she designed the ADU to accommodate changes and modifications.

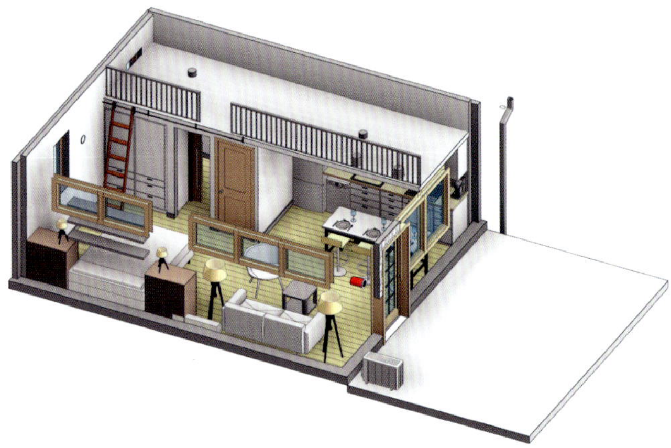

This cozy and cheerful ADU has an open floor plan, which makes it easy for the homeowner to move or swap out furniture depending on how they're using the space.

BROOKLAND 2022

Schinder's clients had recently bought their home and wanted an ADU they could rent out to generate income. Two sides of the structure are bermed—meaning they're below grade and covered by earth—so she added a large window and a double-paned glass door to bring in natural light from the other two sides.

Natural light and reinforced foundations transformed a small, cave-like garage into a bright and modern one-bedroom ADU.

RADICAL FLEXIBILITY

San Diego, California

ARCHITECTS
Ramiro Losada-Amor (Modern Granny Flats) and Prismática Architects

When Jorge and Ruben first decided to move to San Diego to be with aging parents, they looked for a single lot with two small houses. When they couldn't find that, they settled on a traditional family house with a four-car garage.

The garage was an immense unfinished 1,200-square-foot space. It was the perfect blank canvas for the couple, who live dynamic and mobile lives, to picture how they wanted to use the space. "From our earliest conversations they expressed a desire for a space that adapts to their lifestyle," says architect Ramiro Losada-Amor. Teaming up with Prismática Architects, he replaced the concrete floors with cement, installed plumbing, and updated the electrical system for residential use. Then they transformed the interior into an efficient and comfortable ADU.

To break up the garage's rectangular expanse, the team constructed an A-frame structure at the center of the space to house the bathroom, the plumbing part of the kitchen, and storage areas. The rest of the space is open, with moving and folding elements that enable different areas to be quickly and easily changed and reconfigured depending on the needs of each moment.

Because Jorge often works from home, a mobile partition can divide the bedroom into two separate spaces—one for working and one that still functions as a sleeping area. Furniture on wheels, built-in shelving, and cleverly stored seating allow the living/kitchen area to be used for a variety of purposes, from entertaining and relaxing to yoga or working out to hosting a meeting or work session. The number of people staying in the house also changes. Sometimes one of them is home, sometimes both, and other times they host guests. When that's the case, a Murphy bed integrated into a bookcase converts the living room into a guest bedroom. "They wanted radical flexibility," says Losada-Amor, "opportunities to use the spaces exactly how they wanted to."

The completed project works well for his clients. They love their modern, versatile ADU, and their parents love their traditional house. "The space can adapt for how they'll be living over the next twenty years," says Losada-Amor. "It's perfect."

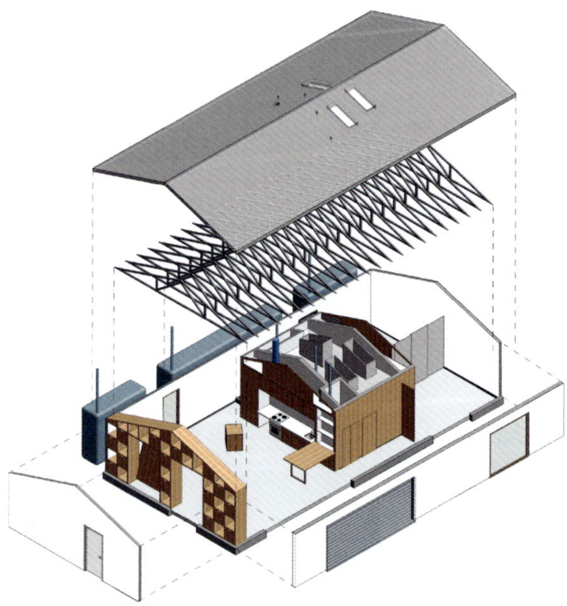

To break up the rectangular expanse, Losada-Amor set an A-frame structure at the center to hold the bathroom, the kitchen plumbing, and storage areas.

The open, flexible space flows around the interior A-frame box, with the bathroom enclosed in the center.

An A-frame structure at the center of the space encloses the bathroom, the plumbing part of the kitchen, and storage areas, leaving the space around it open.

Sliding walls and partitions open or close off spaces as needed.

AGING IN PLACE: DESIGNING ADUS TO AGE WITH US

Wide hallways and sliding doors are easier to navigate through as we age. Windows and skylights on multiple walls provide different qualities of light and air flow.

"There's a huge need for housing that can accommodate our aging population," says Bay Area–based architect Carrie Shores Diller. Since California relaxed its regulations on ADU building in 2018, she and her firm, Inspired ADUs, have designed more than two hundred ADUs, many for clients hoping to "age in place." It's a concept that has gained significant traction over the past few years, reflecting our aging population's desire to remain in their own homes or communities rather than moving into an assisted living facility or with their grown children. "ADUs are a great opportunity to design with aging in mind," says Diller.

While 90 percent of older Americans prefer to age at home, a 2020 report estimated that less than 10 percent of homes are "aging-ready," which is defined by a step-free entryway, a bedroom and bathroom on the first floor, and at least one bathroom accessibility feature (e.g., grab bars or handrails).

Aging-in-place design is firmly rooted in the principles of universal design, an inclusive design philosophy focused on creating environments that can be accessed and used by all people, regardless of their age, size, or abilities. Each principle contains guidelines for designing places and products that are safe and comfortable for as many people as possible.

Many products and spaces are now designed with these principles. A great example is OXO's vegetable peeler, conceived by the company's founder, Sam Farber, in the late 1980s. His wife had trouble using an old-fashioned peeler because of arthritis in her hands, so he designed a better one.

When Diller designs ADUs with aging in mind, she follows the principles of universal design but layers in features and details that are specific to aging. "As our bodies age, they change and may need additional support," she says. "Aging-in-place design can support these changes and keep us independent. It's about designing for how we actually live and age."

When designing an ADU for aging in place, Diller advises her clients to consider:

→ **Orientation:** How much privacy versus connection do you want with the main house?

→ **Accessibility:** How can we make it easy and safe to navigate within and around the ADU? How can we store and organize items so they're easy to find and use?

→ **Light:** How can we place windows, doors, and skylights to take advantage of natural light?

→ **Materials:** Build with materials that are safe, efficient, durable, and beautiful.

ORIENTATION

You can orient your ADU to encourage connection with the rest of the property, provide privacy, or do some of both. Think about what makes the most sense for your own situation but consider that things may change in the future.

- → To encourage connection, face the ADU toward the other house and use the area in between for shared outdoor space.
- → For privacy, angle the ADU away from the house. You might lose outdoor space, but you can add private paths, patios, and decks.
- → Pathways, landscaping, and trellises can create separate private spaces.
- → Leaving outdoor space around the perimeter of the ADU makes the living area feel larger and promotes indoor/outdoor connection.

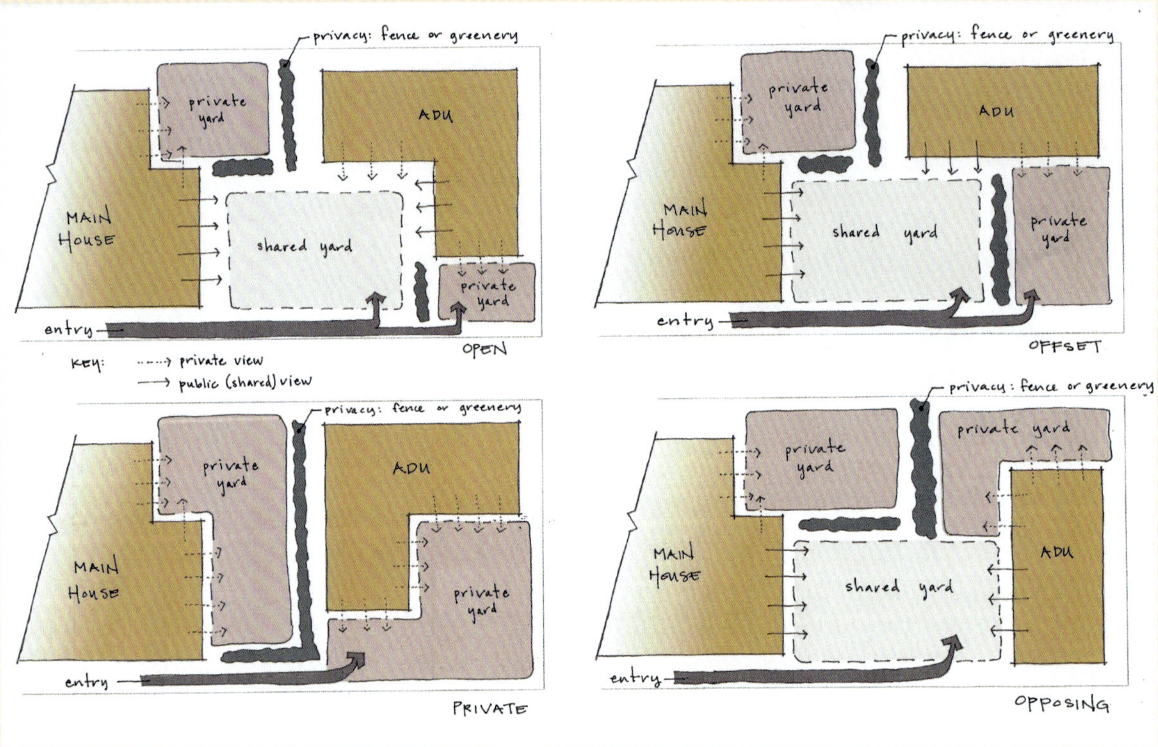

The ADU is strategically positioned behind the main house to provide a balance of privacy and connection. Separate or communal spaces are created with landscaping and outdoor living areas.

ACCESSIBILITY

Design your ADU so that the things you do or use the most are convenient and accessible. This includes moving between indoor and outdoor spaces, navigating inside the ADU, and storing what you use often in "the reach zone" where it's easy to access.

above
Large openings, wide hallways, and sliding doors make it easier to navigate internal spaces and foster indoor/outdoor connection.

left
Place appliances (like this paneled microwave and dishwasher) under the counter to avoid needing to reach overhead. Cabinets on both sides of the kitchen peninsula add reachable storage space.

above
Creative pullout storage solutions maximize reachable cabinet space.

left
Bench seating and intentional placement of furniture can save space and add storage.

LIGHT

On any building site, our understanding of the position of the sun and prevailing wind patterns allows us to take advantage of cross ventilation and natural light, considered the best light for aging eyes. We can strategically add windows and doors to maximize light and air flow; we can angle the ADU to receive direct morning or direct afternoon light.

As we get older, the muscles that control our reaction to light and pupil size begin to lose their strength, and our eyes become less responsive to changes in lighting. Without proper lighting support, this can strain eye muscles and even affect circadian rhythms and sleeping habits. Optimal lighting for aging eyes incorporates multiple light sources. They complement one another to create a balanced space:

→ Natural light is best for our eyes, but it's important to avoid glare;
→ Task lighting highlights a specific area—such as over the kitchen sink or the bathroom vanity;
→ LED lights are energy efficient and have a high color rendering index (CRI), which means they show colors more accurately and clearly.

opposite
Corner windows bring in more light and extend the interior space to the outside.

right
Light sources from various directions help the space feel bigger. Glass entry doors add natural light and provide visual connection to the outdoors from any height.

below
Clerestory windows provide privacy while bringing in fresh air and a sense of the weather.

MATERIALS

Building ADUs gives us the opportunity to design sustainable and safe living spaces. It's important to source furnishings and finishes to limit off-gassing, the airborne release of chemicals from materials into the built environment. Our bodies' ability to handle off-gassing diminishes greatly as we age, so make sure to check the details and specifications of materials you bring into the home. Certain plywoods, for example, use stains and adhesives that off-gas volatile organic compounds (VOCs), causing unhealthy air quality.

Induction cooktops add another layer of safety because they remain cool to the touch (they only heat the area touching the cookware).

left
New construction allows you to avoid steps or awkward transitions between rooms and into/out of showers. Make sure floor the materials have the proper amount of friction between the surfaces to achieve zero threshold transitions and curbless showers.

above
Contrasting colors and materials helps orient the space and helps the eyes focus on different planes.

right
Place showerheads at various heights and include a handheld shower head—great for washing the shower or a dog. Choose faucets, handles, and other fixtures that require minimal grip strength.

HIDDEN STUDIO

Coopers Shoot, New South Wales, Australia

ARCHITECT
Harley Graham (HGA Studio)

In 2017, Australian architect Harley Graham (HGA Studio) was approached by a couple who lived on a twenty-acre property in Coopers Shoot. Just south of Byron Bay, it is a small rural community known for its lush, rolling hills and panoramic views.

The couple had owned the property for twenty-two years. When they decided to retire and live there full-time, they asked Graham to design a private guesthouse for friends and family. "They wanted something completely separate from the main house," Graham says. "A self-sufficient guest pavilion."

The two existing buildings on the property—the couple's home and a writing cabin—were designed by the late Ian McKay. McKay was part of the Sydney School, a group of unconventional architects active in the 1950s and 1960s. Sydney School architects were heavily influenced by American architects like Frank Lloyd Wright and John Lautner. They embraced organic design

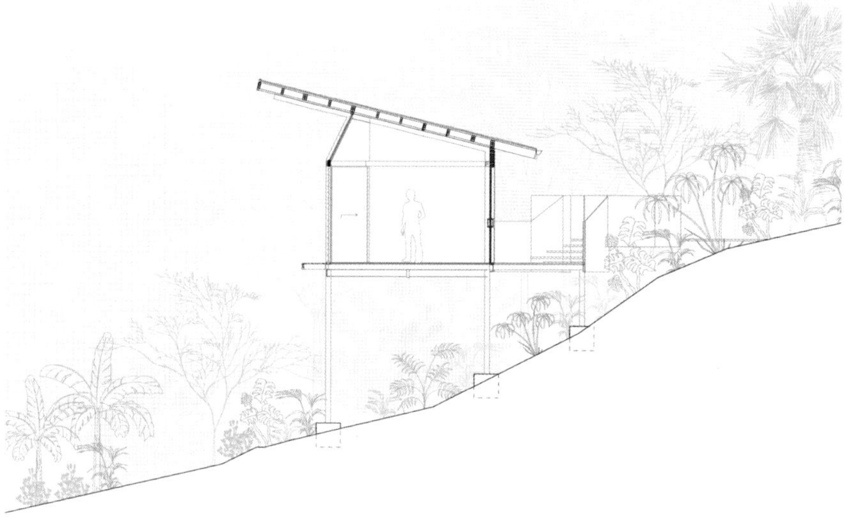

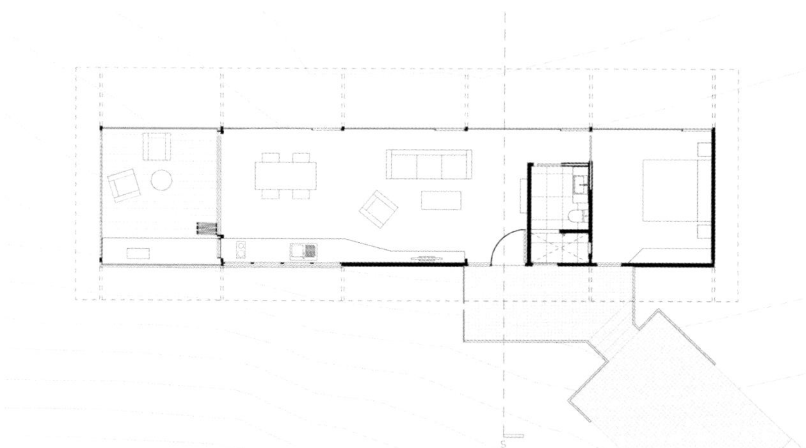

Architect sketches show how the ADU integrates into the natural surroundings, nestled into the trees on a steep slope and accessed on the higher side by a steel bridge built into the hillside.

Perched among the trees, the ADU looks over farmland, rolling hills, and the ocean beyond.

principles, using local materials and focusing on integrating design with the surrounding environment. "They did lots of climate sensitive design," says Graham. "They were kind of a bunch of hippies who became quite well-known and went on to lead prestigious design firms."

With Hidden Studio, Graham paid tribute to McKay's other designs on the property. "They provided guiding principles and set rules for what this building could be," Graham says. "We stood on the shoulders of a hero." In keeping with McKay's approach of exposing structural elements, the repeated exposed portal frames reveal the building's design without hidden components, presenting a clear and pared-back form.

Hidden Studio blends seamlessly into its environment, softened by the hills and surrounding foliage. Its restrained color and material palette reflects the inherent simplicity. Positioned to capture northern light, louver blinds allow cool winds to ventilate the space during warmer months. Large plate glass windows along the front frame views of the Coopers Shoot hills and the ocean beyond.

opposite and above
Hidden Studio pays homage to the legacy of accomplished local architect Ian McKay, known for his organic design principles, which expose and celebrate the natural beauty of a building's structural components. Nestled into the hill on a sprawling twenty-acre property in Coopers Shoot, New South Wales, Hidden Studio complements the main house and the writer's cabin on the property—both designed by McKay. "Respecting the existing structures on-site was key," says architect Harley Graham.

overleaf
The ADU has unobstructed views of the surrounding countryside with the ocean in the distance.

Vancouver, Canada

DESIGN
Smallworks, with MAAS Architecture

UPLIFT

Uplift is a collaboration between award-winning Canadian architect Marianne Amodio and Vancouver-based design-build firm Smallworks. It was designed for a client who practices an exercise therapy called the Feldenkrais Method. She wanted a quiet space to teach and practice that could double as a part-time home for her two daughters when they visit from out of town.

Built in 2014, the bright, open studio is an embodiment of the client's work in Feldenkrais, which is like yoga but with an emphasis on small, directed movements. Exposed rafters soar overhead like a series of vertebrae, representing the spine's role in movement and bodywork. "The structure is like a skeleton," says Jake Fry, founder and principal of Smallworks. "It's ever present in what you see." The unusual skewed roofline, sloped and on a cross axis, accentuates the importance of structure—in physical buildings, our bodies, and as a lifestyle concept. "The organic structure is the most present element of this home," Fry says.

Intentionally plain and uncluttered, the studio provides an undisturbed canvas for practicing Feldenkrais. At the same time, it easily transforms into a comfortable and fully equipped living space, with a Murphy bed, a bay window seat, and sliding doors along the west wall that open to a private garden. "Everything is hidden," Fry says. "It's a clinical, high-gloss environment but you turn around and it converts into this other space."

The intentionally understated studio gets noticed for its unusual skewed roofline and a pop of bright yellow on the outside panel.

The ADU transitions seamlessly from a peaceful minimalistic retreat to a fully equipped living space. Almost every visible face along the south and east walls conceals features and/or storage options.

DESERT RETREAT

Yucca Valley, California

ARCHITECT
Oonagh Ryan (ORA)

This bright and peaceful studio ADU sits on a five-acre site just outside the town of Yucca Valley in California's high desert. Purchased as a weekend retreat by a family from Los Angeles in 2014, the secluded spot is surrounded by acres of undeveloped land protected by the Bureau of Land Management.

The family had planned to remodel the existing structures on the property, but upon inspection the unpermitted buildings were condemned by the local building inspector. Instead of attempting to upgrade them to meet current building codes, the owners decided to rebuild. They hired the Los Angeles–based architecture firm ORA to design two independent structures—a home and an ADU with a garage.

Building these structures while adhering to her client's brief, which stated that "no existing rocks or trees were to be disturbed and new structures were to blend into the land," was

The two structures needed to fit within the existing boulders and trees and blend into the landscape.

"an exercise in geometric precision," says principal architect Oonagh Ryan. The land was covered with immense native rock formations. Despite the large parcel size, it was challenging to find the space.

Over the next two years, Ryan and her team meticulously designed the two structures, strategically placing openings to bring natural light and air deep into the rooms. They added decks and patios so that each space has its own unique relationship with the dramatic landscape. The main house, a single-story, three-bedroom cabin, is nestled in between several large rock outcroppings. The two-story ADU contains a 254-square-foot studio that provides flexible space for work or guests. It bridges over the rock formations, connecting directly to nearby hiking trails. On the ground floor is a single-car garage with laundry, storage, and room for the home-owner's vintage teardrop camper—which serves as an extra bedroom when needed.

left
Underneath the ADU is a single-car garage.

below
Architectural sketch shows how the main house and the ADU are carefully positioned among the rocks and trees.
1. entry
2. kitchen
3. living/dining area
4. primary bedroom
5. primary bathroom
6. bedroom
7. bathroom
8. living/dining/bedroom area
9. deck
10. patio
11. parking

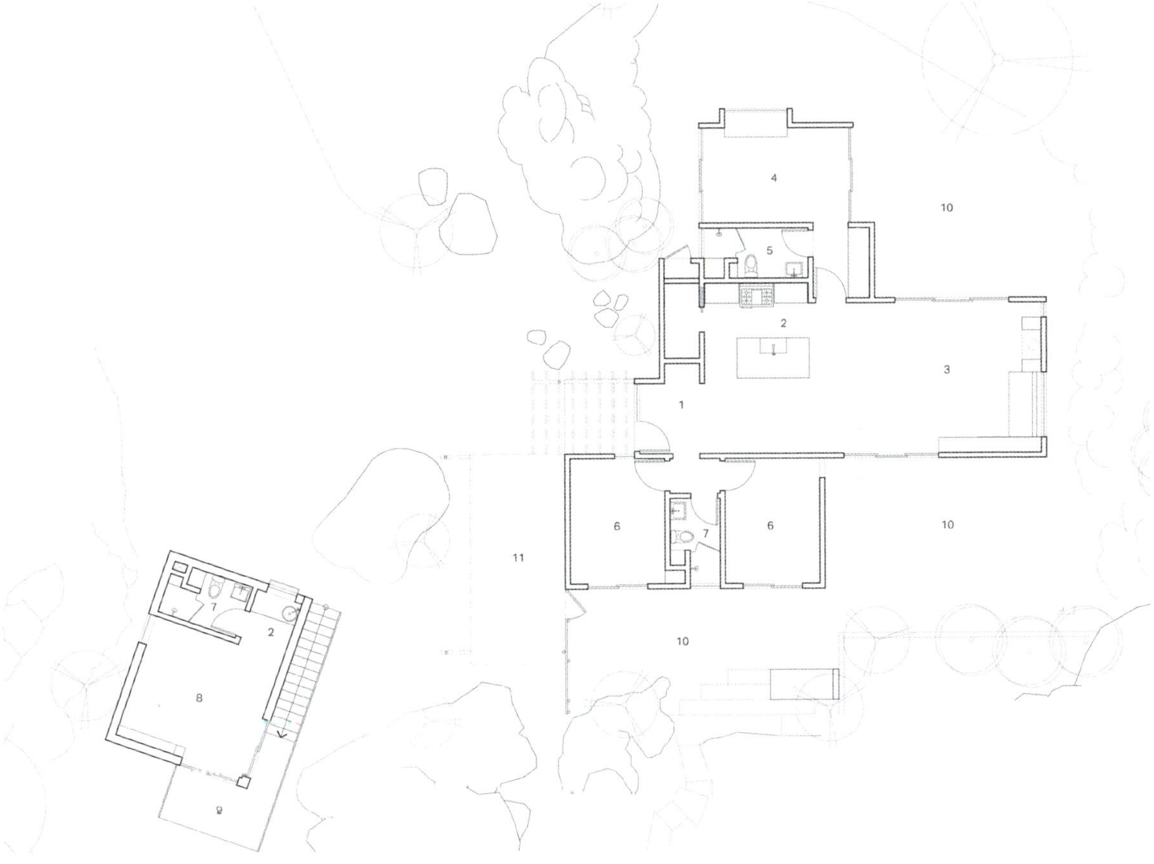

above and opposite top
When not in use, a custom queen-size Murphy bed is concealed inside a birch plywood cabinet that includes a storage closet on one side.

oppsite bottom
Strategically placed windows capture the views of immense ancient rock formations. Natural materials and colors, including green linoleum and birch plywood, pull the outdoor environment inside.

Minimal furnishings and soothing colors create a sense of tranquility inside the compact space.

Factory seconds from Heath Ceramics create unique and distinct patterns and color stories in all the bathrooms. In the ADU, the colors work in harmony with the vibrant green linoleum floor.

BIRDHOUSE

Austin, Texas

ARCHITECT
Francisco Arredondo
(North Arrow Studio)

PROJECT MANAGER
Bobbie Behm
(North Arrow Studio)

"There's something about Birdhouse that triggers a collective memory," says Austin-based architect Francisco Arredondo. "It's like the little drawing that everyone makes as a kid when you're told to draw a house."

Birdhouse is located in Chestnut, an old and established East Austin neighborhood with tree-lined streets and modest single-story bungalows from the 1940s and 1950s. Arredondo's client had purchased a 5,900-square-foot lot that included the original bungalow in the front, plus a yard with alley access in the back. She wanted to add a two-bedroom ADU that she could use as a rental property.

Arredondo's first challenge was Austin's housing code, which capped development at "either 1,100 square feet or .15 floor area ratio (FAR) of the lot, whichever is smaller." This left him only 886 square feet (5,908-square-foot lot × .15 FAR = 886 square feet). The code also said that while adding a garage wasn't required, the additional space wouldn't count against the FAR. By including a garage—which can be seamlessly integrated into the home's existing interior—Arredondo added a valuable 200 square feet of living space to the property.

Another challenge was the three pecan trees on the property, classified as protected by the City of Austin Tree Ordinance. "You can't cut them and there are additional development restrictions around them," Arredondo says. "They regulate how close you can build, how many branches you can cut, and the square footage of impact to the root system." By designing Birdhouse in an L shape, Arredondo was able to squeeze the residence between the three trees, highlighting the 21-foot tree in the center of the property. "We were pinned in," he said. "There literally wasn't anywhere else it could go."

Arredondo designed Birdhouse to fit the scale of the structures around it. He chose corrugated metal for the main building material as a nod to the small sheds, carports, and other simple structures that neighbors along the alley had

"We love round windows. We try to sneak them into projects whenever we can." —Francisco Arredondo

built for themselves over the years, most likely from extra material they had left over from a roof. "We wanted to reference some of the vernacular architecture of the neighborhood," he says. "Corrugated metal is also relatively inexpensive and versatile; you can use it for the walls and the roof." To inject what he refers to as "an extra design intention," he added a series of round windows throughout the two-story structure. "It's a way to contrast the simple shape with something playful and whimsical," he says.

Completed in 2022, Arredondo says that Birdhouse is his favorite of the more than twenty ADUs he's designed in the Austin area so far. "I used to describe this house as 'an exercise in simplicity carried to the extreme,'" he says. "But in the end, it's just a smart little house that makes people smile."

Circular windows are found throughout the house. Egress codes require an operable window in each bedroom, so one window swings out. "We found out the hard way that it's very unusual to do an operable round window that also meets egress requirements," Arredondo says. "It was a lot of trial and error." He eventually decided on an "offset hinge design," with a fixed panel on the right side for the hinge. The glass has a little circular door handle at the end.

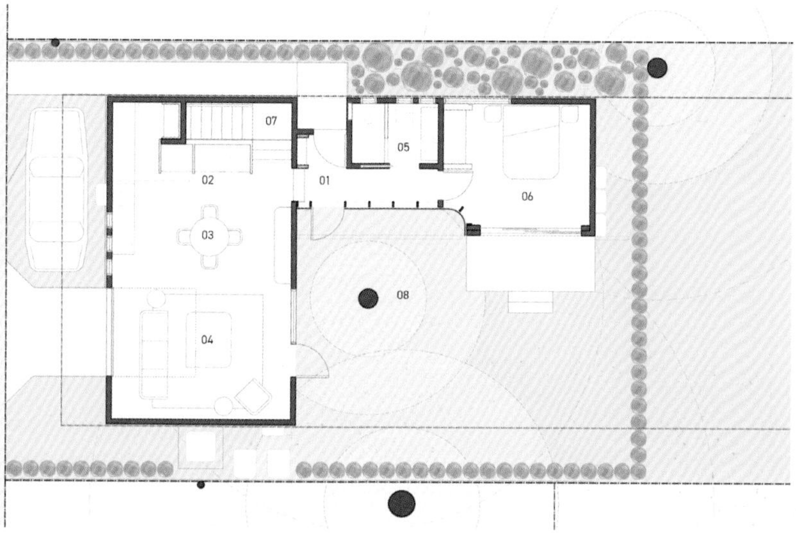

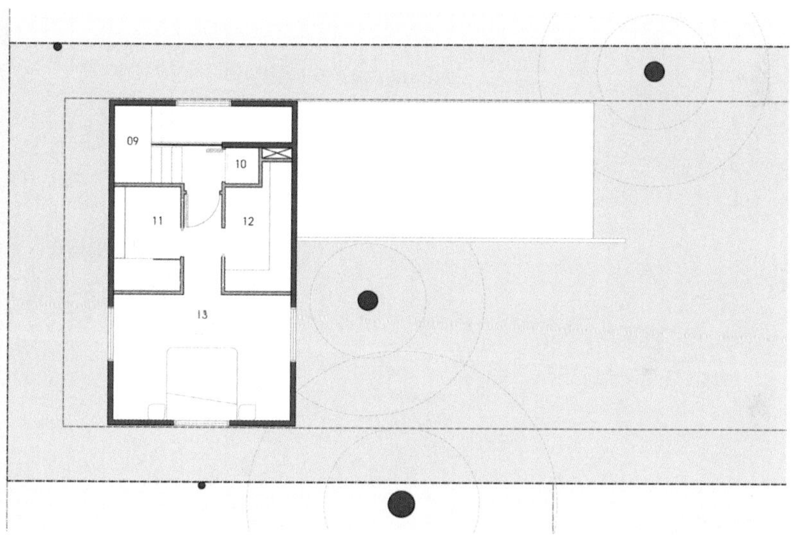

opposite
The L-shaped orientation allows Birdhouse to squeeze between three protected pecan trees on the property. In Austin, if a tree's diameter is 19 inches or larger, it's considered protected. If it's 24 inches or larger in diameter and of a certain species, it's a heritage tree.

above
The circles around the trees represent "spheres of influence." Inside the first circle, you can't develop at all. Inside the second circle, you can only disturb up to 4 inches of soil. The largest circle is "full critical root zone," and you can only disturb up to 50 percent of the overall root zone.

01. entry
02. kitchen
03. dining
04. living
05. bathroom 01
06. bedroom 01
07. stairs
08. courtyard
09. stairs
10. laundry
11. primary bathroom
12. primary closet
13. primary bedroom

above
Including a garage added 200 square feet of interior space.

opposite
The private outdoor space centers around an enormous pecan tree.

Seattle, Washington

ARCHITECTURE AND DESIGN
Joe Schneider and Michael Freeman, JAS Design Build

JEWEL BOX

Located in the Queen Anne neighborhood of Seattle, Jewel Box was designed in 2017 for a retired homeowner who wanted to travel and rent out his main residence. "He was making it for himself," says designer Michael Freeman of JAS Design Build. "He wanted a sweet little place to stay when he was in town."

At only 500 square feet, Jewel Box is the smallest ADU that JAS has designed. It has a kitchen and dining area overlooking a private patio on the lower level, and a bedroom/living room with a bathroom above. At the time, ADU zoning laws in Seattle were extremely restrictive, limiting square footage based on lot size. "This lot was very tight," Freeman says. "We played all kinds of games to get the most out of it that we could."

Because one side of the original garage runs along the property line, the upper level had to be moved over about 2 feet to comply with the fire code. "Historically, garages were allowed to run along the property line, but those rules have changed," Freeman explains. "Any new additions need to comply with the current code." To make up for lost space, he bumped the opposite side of the upper floor over as well, so it hangs over the lower level. "The interesting thing about these ADUs is that you have to run all the numbers first," Freeman says. "Once you've done that, it's more like putting together a puzzle that's already solved."

With two-level ADUs, Freeman says the challenge is where to put the stairs, which still need to meet standard-sized code requirements. "They take up so much space," he says. "Start there, then think where you have room to flex and push the boundaries." In Jewel Box, the stairs cut into the ceiling space of the garage to ensure the required head height.

They also pushed boundaries along the gable roofline, where they inserted a series of pop-up dormers that add height and volume to sections

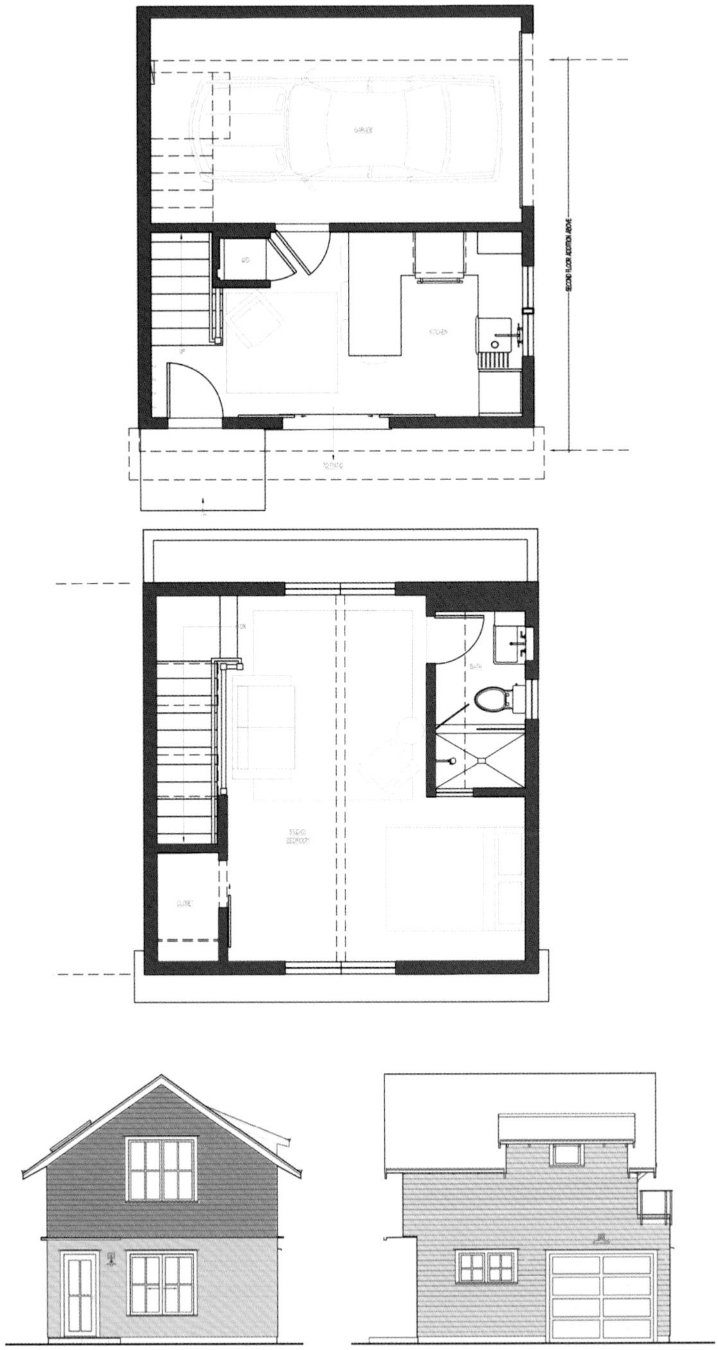

Site plan of the lot details the size restrictions.

A wall of sliding windows stretches the lower level by connecting the kitchen/dining space to a private courtyard.

of the sidewalls. "That's where the bathroom is," Freeman says. "It feels like you're inside a cabinet."

While he recognizes that this type of restricted design is "less conventional," Freeman, who lives in an 800-square-foot ADU he built himself, believes there's something uniquely satisfying about these quirky little homes. "People think it'll feel too cramped, but when they occupy these spaces, it's actually really nice," he says. "There's a comfort in being cradled by the building."

Freeman says that interest in ADUs has grown steadily since the city legalized them in 2009. JAS has built a handful over the years, ranging in size up to 800 square feet, which until recently was the maximum size allowed by code. (Code revisions have increased that to 1,000 square feet.) "These are interesting design problems because they make you reconsider what we really 'need' to live comfortably," Freeman says. "And from a larger perspective, they offer another option to help Seattle address housing shortages and affordability."

top
To ensure the required head height, the stairs cut into the ceiling space of the garage.

bottom
The designers tucked the bathroom into a pop-up dormer. An interior window called a relite brings light in from multiple directions and makes the small room feel more spacious. Exposed and painted paneling (Benjamin Moore's Intrigue) adds texture and personality to the upper level.

Skylights pull natural light down the stairwell, lighting the lower level as well.

INSIDE ADDITION

Mill Valley, California

ARCHITECT
Whitney Schrauth (SA+C Inc.)

What began as unusable space under architect Whitney Schrauth's five-bedroom house is now enjoying its third life, transformed from a damp, dark basement into a functioning and efficient ground floor addition, and then again into a spacious and bright two-bedroom ADU.

Phase One: When Schrauth embarked on a major renovation of her 3,140-square-foot house in 2011, she needed a new foundation. To keep the existing footprint and floor levels above in place, they held the house up on cribbing and dug 2 feet down to pour a new perimeter foundation. A concrete slab throughout the new lower level was designed to double as the finished floor. With the newfound space, Schrauth carved out an office, bathroom, kitchenette, laundry room, and storage space, and connected the floors with an internal staircase. "It served our needs at that time," she says.

Phase Two: When California changed the zoning laws in 2018 to make it easier for homeowners to add ADUs to their homes, Schrauth claimed more space and converted the lower level into an ADU. "We took a lot of the space we'd been using for storage and turned it into living space," she says. "What used to be a two-car garage became a one-car garage and a guest bedroom; the hallway is full of creative storage solutions."

Schrauth meticulously designed the ADU as a flexible, multipurpose space. It has everything it needs to serve as a private living space, yet the configuration makes it easy to block off certain areas or rooms to be used for different purposes. Her spacious office, with direct access to a private patio, includes a sizable closet, should its next purpose be a primary bedroom. The "workshop" in the garage can double as just a garage.

Schrauth says there are many ways she could envision using the space in the future: Maybe her kids could live there after college or she could move down there herself as she ages. They could also rent it out. "Having an ADU is like an exercise in flexibility," she says. "It's added so much value to our home."

top
Separate private passage from ADU to street.

bottom
Private patio for ADU.

opposite
Schrauth designed her office to maximize light and views of the outdoors. She also included two closets and custom built-in storage so the room could easily serve as a primary bedroom.

SA
+C
architecture
+ lifestyle
www.saandc.com
415.888.8604

above
Schrauth takes advantage of valuable "shallow storage" spaces throughout the ADU: Open bookshelves in the bedroom are built into otherwise wasted space in the stud walls.

left
A closet with shelves and hooks is created from unused space in the hallway and concealed by a sliding barn door.

top
Schrauth created an open loop in-floor heating system that runs the hot water from her sinks upstairs through the concrete floor first. "The heating is radiant by design," she says. "It's efficient and healthy and there's no dust."

bottom
Living room/flex space can be sealed off with sliding barn doors.

THE FUTURE (IS HERE)

The IT House uses a flexible building system that is fabricated off-site and assembled on-site. The efficient and minimal aluminum and glass structure is available in six different plans and designed to achieve a high level of functionality within a small footprint.

As the "new normal" merges into, simply, "the normal," we're more comfortable with a revised definition of home. Traditional values like stability, continuity, and permanence aren't relevant in a lifestyle dependent on resilience, flexibility, and adaptability. We're also facing a global reckoning on space—specifically, the difference between how much space we feel entitled to and the space we actually need. Regulations are adapting as well, recognizing changes in lifestyle and a demographic shift from large family households to single-person and smaller family units.

Addressing the housing crisis and creating sustainable housing are global priorities. For architects and builders, residential design offers an opportunity to collaborate with scientists, doctors, engineers, and entrepreneurs to address questions from an interdisciplinary perspective: What do we really need from our homes? How can our homes enhance our lives?

Once we embrace this mindset, the term "ADU" feels limiting. ADUs are an important introduction to "infill architecture," but we can do so much more. In Edmonton, Canada, mini-neighborhoods are emerging in previously underutilized alleyways, where garages are transformed into small homes. In Europe, sustainable "conscious communities" prioritize flexibility and respond dynamically to residents' housing needs. But it starts with the ADU.

THE IT HOUSE

ARCHITECT: LINDA TAALMAN (TAALMAN ARCHITECTURE)

"It starts with the ADU," says architect Linda Taalman. "When people see them, they think, 'I could totally live here.' And they could totally live there. We could all totally live there." Over the past few years, she and her Los Angeles–based team at Taalman Architecture have been developing a building typology for ADUs. Available in six standard plans, the IT House shares a "design language" of components, materials, and systems.

IT Houses are minimal aluminum-and-glass structures with small footprints. "They're simple containers that give you insulation and big openings for expansive views," Taalman says. Constructed off-site, the materials are assembled in synchronized and integrated layers on-site. "It's fewer steps, fewer materials, and less scale," she says. "Less is less."

IT Houses were designed for remote sites, small lots, or urban environments. The ADUs were intentionally designed to replace existing accessory buildings such as carports and garages without compromising access to exterior spaces. "With the ADUs, we knew how tight some of these sites were going to be," Taalman says. "Having a really small footprint was key." The units range in size from a 300-square-foot studio (the Pod) to a 1,200-square-foot three-bedroom. In between there are the 360-square-foot Box (to replace the two-car garage), the two-story Cube, and the tall, skinny Tower. "Even if you think you don't have enough space, you can squeeze this one in," Taalman says.

So far, Taalman Architecture has built twelve IT ADUs throughout greater Los Angeles: seven Cubes, two Boxes, two Towers, and one Pod.

They're also prototyping the 1,200-square-foot model as a single-family dwelling in the high desert. Taalman says she's excited about all the projects, but her goals have changed. "In the beginning, I wanted to see hundreds of new housing units in the city," she says. "But with how the laws are changing, there are opportunities to make a much bigger impact."

Los Angeles has already started incentivizing homeowners to build more than one ADU on their property. They're also relaxing the rules around ADU placement—now the "primary" house can be in the front, back, or middle of the property and you can add an 800-square-foot ADU pretty much anywhere on your lot. "I saw this vision of how our cities can be," Taalman says. "Every lot that's zoned for a single-family house should be able to incorporate two more units."

In 2024, Taalman bought an empty lot in East LA. "I decided if I really wanted to show the full potential of what is possible, I need to do it myself," she says. Her goal is to create a "small footprint development" of three two-story units, all under 1,000 square feet. "I want a new way of doing it that is much more friendly," she says. "I don't want fences between these units. I want to be able to hang out with my neighbor and hang out with my family." She plans to keep the interiors as open as possible. "It's like a two-story living space," she says. "A big, open space that you can add separations and divisions to if you want."

Taalman sees this project as a proof of concept for anyone wondering how three people can cohabit. She's grappling with an endless list of questions—from the tangible (how do we think about rooms? internal layouts? indoor versus outdoor spaces?) to the environmental (how big is our footprint? integrate solar? close all the loops on the water and energy nexus?) to the philosophical (how do we really want to live today?). "This prototype is like a case study to start thinking about these things," she says.

Taalman's first hurdle is financial. How do you make good design affordable? "It's not about what looks good in a magazine but understanding what people actually need from their homes," she says. "What's going to give people quality of life experiences? What's going to elevate their lives? A very reductive, simple house with good light, good proportions, and nice-sized, operable windows with access to exterior space can meet those needs."

Taalman says her ultimate goal is to change how we think about building new communities. "The key is designing a language of systems and components that you can reconfigure and tailor for different sites," she says. "It's like we're giving you a really smart way of thinking about it, and you can take it as far as you want."

THE WELL LIVING LAB: CAN OUR HOMES IMPROVE OUR HEALTH?

ROCHESTER, MINNESOTA
ARCHITECTS: CSA IN PARTNERSHIP WITH THE MAYO CLINIC

In 2022, architects Christopher Strom and Isaiah Scharen of CSA partnered with the Mayo Clinic to design the Well Living Lab, a two-bedroom house tricked out with mechanical components to allow researchers to study the impact of the indoor environment on health and well-being. Research participants would live in the house for certain periods of time, while being watched and monitored from the clinic two blocks away.

Each space within the 700-square-foot unit was intentionally designed to encourage participants to focus on specific activities. "The layout follows the activities across the day," says Scharen. "The bedroom faces east where the sun rises, and the office is in the middle, and spaces where people are cooking and doing more leisure activities are on the west side." As participants move through the house, researchers can test the impact of different products and activities on air quality. A mechanical closet in the back of the unit allows researchers to access and tend the electrical systems without entering the residence.

Testing how different kinds of light can affect our eyes and our overall quality of life required a baseline of total darkness, which the architects achieved by installing two types of electronically retractable shading to every window and skylight: an opaque but translucent filtering shade and a full blackout shade. Both rolls are locked into side channels so that light can't seep around the edges. "It's unusual to invest that much in blackout and privacy shades in such a small unit because there's not much room for the pocketing of those systems," says Strom. "It forced us to be really disciplined and precise about how to integrate all this technology and amenities into such a small package. Having done it once, now we can bring that to our other projects."

How do you design something smaller without feeling like it's a compromise? "Building smaller is just another level of constraints," says Strom. "Once you've figured out a way to meet the size restrictions, you can achieve so much more."

The Well Living Lab combines structural engineering and health sciences to create a space for scientists to study how different environmental factors affect people within a home setting.

San Diego's Bonus Program allows homeowners to build multiple ADUs on single-family lots. From the street, you can hardly see that the modest house on the left is the same property as the multi-unit development visible opposite.

THE DENSITY INCENTIVE

SAN DIEGO, CALIFORNIA

In 2021, the city of San Diego added a provision to their ADU ordinance called the Bonus Program. If a homeowner adds one "deed-restricted" ADU to their property—in this case, "deed-restricted" means it will be rented as low- or middle-income housing for at least fifteen years—they can build a second, or "bonus," ADU and rent it at market rate.

Throughout urban San Diego, homeowners are using the Bonus Program to add multiple ADUs to single-family lots. The program allows two bonus ADUs on top of what's normally allowed, and even more if the property is close to public transit. With almost half of them renting at below market rates, over the last three years San Diego has created more affordable ADUs than the rest of California combined. "Rather than a financial incentive, it's a 'density incentive,'" explains Jared Basler, director of policy and strategic initiatives for the California housing nonprofit Casita Coalition. "You could build one, but if you deed restrict it, you could build two."

Despite its success in boosting the local housing supply, not all San Diego residents are in favor of the Bonus Program. "We're always going to run into people who are under the impression that they bought their neighborhood, not their home," Basler says. "We hear everything from the traditional 'they should do it in other neighborhoods' to 'I'll never see a sunrise again if there's an ADU blocking my view.' Whatever it is, it's disappointing, because at the end of the day we need the housing, period."

What concerns Basler more than local opposition is the lack of skilled labor, an issue he thinks will plateau ADU building in the next three to four years. "We can't keep growing at the rate we have simply because there aren't enough people who can build them," he says. "We're desperately behind on skilled labor."

Another issue is the limited capacity within the electric grid. Each time a new unit is built, the electric company has to check whether there's enough power in the existing lines. If there's not, they need to upgrade the infrastructure, costing

the homeowner up to $50,000 and creating more strain on the existing grid. "The cost of upgrading at the same time that we're removing our ability to offset natural gas is creating a bottleneck in the electric grid," Basler says. "We could have people who want to build in every backyard and all the labor to do it, but if we don't have the capacity set up in the grid to support it, the project will die."

Even so, San Diego's Bonus Program is making national headlines and challenging cities across the country to consider more creative solutions for their housing crises. "We'll continue to work on the technical barriers and the messaging to remind people about the benefits of ADUs," Basler says. "And we'll continue to remind the legislature why they're so important." He also considers ADUs just one of many tools for building more affordable housing, along with townhouses, cottage courts, and lot splits. "It's taken seven years to get where we are now with ADUs and there's a lot of excitement for what's next," he says. "It's really about giving new typologies and processes time to marinate and time for the expertise to grow into it."

9736A

Canada

BUILDER
Honomobo

LANEWAY CULTURE

Before founding Honomobo, Daniel Engelman was building custom homes in Edmonton, Canada. It was all infill architecture, meaning he was knocking down older homes and replacing them with newer, bigger ones. The problem with this model was its effect on the city's housing stock. "You have your million-dollar homes next to your $300,000 homes that are waiting to be torn down," he says. "The people in between were getting pushed out. They couldn't afford what they wanted or it didn't exist."

In 2016, Engelman received a $20,000 grant from the city to design the first Honomobo. The prototype took months of planning to ensure that the home was designed, engineered, and built to comply with all local building codes. He constructed the steel-framed module off-site in three months, then placed it over his garage in two days—one day to pour the concrete foundation and one to install the structure. The 640-square-foot unit is bright and efficient and has direct access to Engelman's back alley, known in Canada as a "laneway."

Since 2016, Honomobo has installed more than 175 homes across North America. The models are permitted in every state and province, and each home is designed to meet local, state, and provincial building codes. With the laneway ADUs, Engelman says he's adding "hidden density" to established neighborhoods throughout the city. "You can't even see them from the street," he says. "We're creating more housing without changing the makeup or charm of the neighborhood." He's also providing affordable housing stock for the "people in between." "We're creating a diverse housing type so different populations can live in them," he says.

As an additional benefit, Engelman says the cottages are revitalizing and improving urban neighborhoods. Mini-communities are springing up, with residents planting gardens and putting up basketball nets in the previously deserted alleys. "It's allowed those forgotten parts of the city to be more lively," he says. "More eyes on the lane equals less crime."

H02 Edmonton, Alberta, Canada

The first Honomobo, H02, built with two shipping containers and placed over Engelman's garage in Edmonton, Alberta, in 2016.

At 640 square feet, the HO2 includes a full bathroom, laundry, and spacious kitchen/living area. It's available in two different layouts, with either one or two bedrooms.

H03 Kelowna, British Columbia, Canada

The second Honomobo, H03, was installed in 2017 in Kelowna, British Columbia. The modular unit is easy to move or reorient on the property. In this case, the unit is perpendicular from the main house on a corner lot, creating a private patio off the front.

H04+ Edmonton, Alberta, Canada

top
Honomobo H04+ was installed in Edmonton, Alberta, in 2018. The two-bedroom, two-bathroom unit connects to the front entrance on the main floor via an interior private staircase. A one-bedroom suite off the garage has its own entrance.

bottom
Open floor plans and walls of windows create an airy, spacious feel inside the 1,280-square-foot H04, Honomobo's most popular model.

Norway

ARCHITECT
Marianne Borge

THE WOODY CABINS

The Woody Cabins are a series of small wooden cabins designed by Norwegian architect Marianne Borge. All under 750 square feet, the cabins are built with sustainable local materials, handcrafted by local carpenters, and designed to blend in with the physical environment around them. "They have a kind of architectural voice," Borge says. "I want them to inspire others to think about living smaller."

The cabins are the architect's response to the "bigger is better" trend in Norway, where developers are taking over huge swaths of natural landscapes to build the Norwegian version of McMansions. Norwegians have traditionally built small cabins, Borge explains, but these are more like second homes, and the sheer size of them is threatening the natural environment around them. "We have to be more concerned about planning for the future," she says. "Making everything on a smaller scale is an important part of that."

The original Woody (Woody 35) came about in 2010, when Borge's client bought a small piece of land and asked her to design a 35-square-meter (377-square-foot) house. Building something that small that was also livable and elegant was a challenge for the architect. "When you build smaller, the architecture tends to be less interesting," she says. "The complexity occurs through working with the light, the materials, and the flow through the house."

Woody 35 was so well received that Borge started getting requests from other people asking for a Woody cottage on their land. In 2014, she added Woody 15, Woody 50, and Woody 70 to the series. Depending on the site, she can adjust and orient each cottage to take advantage of the views and nature surrounding them. The only thing she won't adjust is the size. "Because they're so small, they're kind of a gem," she says. "I've designed plenty of big houses with swimming pools, but this is where I can have a voice in my field."

above
Woody 15 is a one-room cabin with large glass doors that open to the landscape.

left
Inside Woody 35, the smooth plastered surface contrasts with the more rustic wooden exterior. A ladder leads to a sleeping loft above the fireplace.

Big openings let nature in and take advantage of natural light. When the sun is high, the lower level blocks the sun and keeps the cabin cool. When the sun is low, the cabin is filled with sunlight.

above
The Woody Cabins are designed to fit between hills, boulders, and trees without requiring significant changes to the natural environment. The idea is to build several variations on one lot where they can interact with one another.

opposite
At only 377 square feet, Woody 35 can fit into natural environments without altering the terrain.

The Netherlands

ARCHITECT
Ana Rocha

SLIM FIT

Architect Ana Rocha is challenging people in the Netherlands to "live smaller." Despite the country's long-standing dedication to sustainability, she's worried that the Dutch still want volume. "We don't live as big as in the States," she says. "But given the choice, people would choose a big, freestanding house with a huge yard."

It's a mindset Rocha first encountered ten years ago, when she couldn't find a small house (under 650 square feet) in the city of The Hague. "I wanted to live smaller, but it doesn't exist where I live unless you find an apartment," she says. And while larger homes make sense for families, some 40 percent of Holland's population lives alone.

Rocha started thinking about all these individual households in bedroom communities outside the big cities like Amsterdam or Rotterdam, many of whom commuted two to three hours a day between home and work. If they could live in smaller houses inside the city centers, it would reduce their carbon footprint and they wouldn't need to drive every day. "That's when all the puzzle pieces came together," she says. "The ideal situation is to intensify our cities."

Unfortunately, in Holland's city centers most small lots are occupied by cars. That gave Rocha an idea: What if every office building that had an adjacent parking lot offered ten of their parking spots in exchange for housing? With that, Rocha

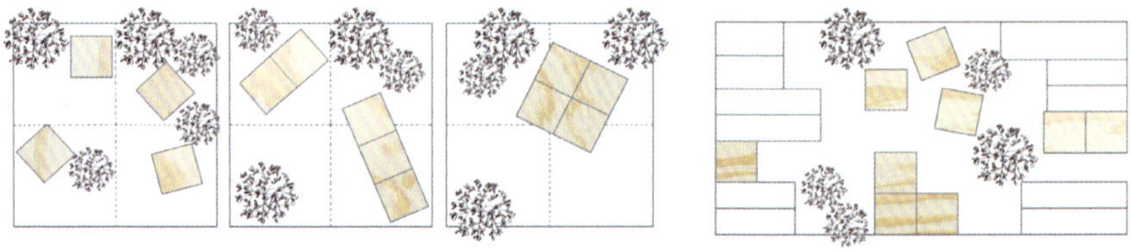

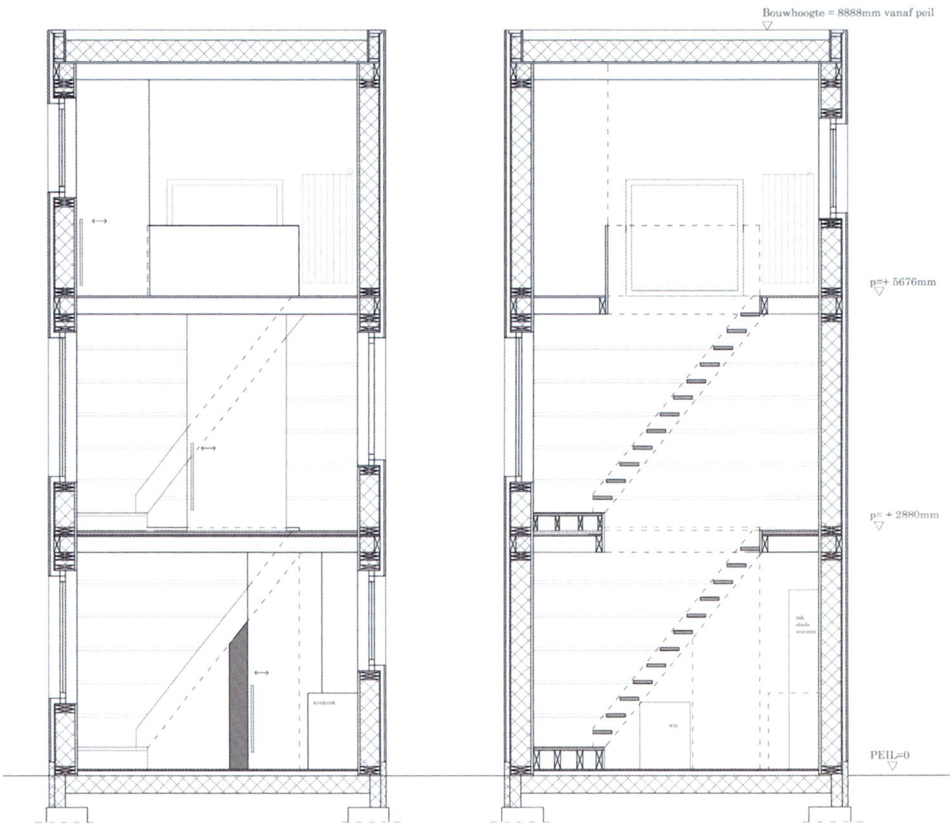

At just under 175 square feet, Slim Fit takes up the same amount of space as two parking spots. It's divided into three levels to accommodate what the architect calls our "three basic needs": cooking/eating, relaxing/sitting, and sleeping (and bathing).

The fixtures and fittings throughout the unit are standard-size, avoiding the extra cost of custom-made items.

challenged herself to design Slim Fit, a 175-square-foot house that takes up the same amount of space as two parking spots. She divided the house into three levels, each dedicated to one of what she calls our "three basic needs": cooking/eating (ground floor), relaxing/sitting (second floor), and sleeping/bathing (third floor). All the internal dimensions, including the stairs, are standard-sized. "I wanted things standard so the furniture didn't need to be custom-made," she says. "You could buy a normal-sized couch or a kitchen from IKEA."

Although she built Slim Fit as a prototype for an urban infill housing unit, Rocha says that Holland isn't ready for that type of project. "This would be the dream, but it's too early here," she says. Real estate developers still make much more money the larger they build, and everything in the city centers is already owned by businesses. Instead, Slim Fit was bought by a company based in Almere, a small city outside Amsterdam. The company hosts foreign collaborators for weeks or months at a time, so buying a house was more cost-effective than putting them up in hotels. "They bought the project while I was still designing it," she says. "So, it's actually not a prototype anymore—it's just a real house."

There's still a long way to go, but Rocha says she's starting to see a change. Cities are beginning to develop residential neighborhoods and carving out a certain number of smaller lots specifically for smaller units. A client of Rocha's bought one of those lots and has commissioned her to build the second Slim Fit. His lot was one of eight designated for small homes. "They sold out immediately and now there's a long waiting list," Rocha says. "My objective isn't really to build one Slim Fit at a time, but it's a very good sign."

Large windows are positioned to bring in the most sunlight and allow for the maximum air flow through the building.

above
Sliding plywood panels can close off the staircase, negating the need for doors between rooms while still offering privacy between the floors. Shelving for books and storage runs up the back wall.

right
The staircase with built-in shelving can be closed off to create privacy or separation between the living area and bedroom above.

Slim Fit was designed for working singles who want to live sustainably and comfortably within dense urban environments.

FEATURED ARCHITECTS AND DESIGNERS

LIL' RED
Oonagh Ryan, ORA
923 East 3rd Street #105
Los Angeles, CA 90013
→ ora.la

GARDEN STUDIO
Harley Graham, HGA Studio
11/18 Banksia Drive
P.O. Box 1285
Byron Bay NSW
2481 Australia
→ hga.studio

MODERN CRAFTSMAN
Hisako Ichiki and Bo Sundius, Bunch Design
837 Foothill Boulevard
La Canada, CA 91011
→ bunchdesign.net

GUEST PAVILION
Jordi Riembau and Miquel Rusca, NordEst Arquitectura
Plaça de la Font, 4
17256 Palau-sator
Girona, Spain
→ nordestarquitectura.com

THE CURVE
Architecture: Navid Masoudi (Mass Builders)
→ navidmasoudi.com
Interior Design: Azadeh Garshasbi (Blend Studio)
→ the-blend.ca

SPACE
Hisako Ichiki and Bo Sundius, Bunch Design
837 Foothill Boulevard
La Canada, CA 91011
→ bunchdesign.net

PASSAGE ISLAND
Honomobo
8603 104 Street NW
Edmonton, AB, T6E 4G6, Canada
→ honomobo.com

ALLEY CAT
Christopher Strom, CSA
3308 Gorham Avenue
St. Louis Park, MN 55426
→ christopherstrom.com

CLOUDVIEW
Loring Sagan and Periscope Homes
The Hearst Building
5 Third Street, 9th Floor
San Francisco, CA 94103
→ bldsf.com

GARAGE MAHAL
Ileana Schinder
7006 MD-195, Office 202
Takoma Park, MD 20912
→ ileanaschinder.com

RADICAL FLEXIBILITY
Ramiro Losada-Amor (Modern Granny Flat) and Prismática Architects
5727 Adelaide Avenue
San Diego, CA 92115
→ moderngrannyflat.com

AGING IN PLACE
Carrie Shores Diller, Inspired ADUs
1220 21st Street
Oakland, CA 94607
→ inspiredadus.com

HIDDEN STUDIO
Harley Graham, HGA Studio
11/18 Banksia Drive
P.O. Box 1285
Byron Bay NSW
2481 Australia
→ hga.studio

UPLIFT
Jake Fry, Smallworks, with MAAS Architecture
#130 - 1639 W. 2nd Avenue
Vancouver, BC, Canada
→ smallworks.ca

DESERT RETREAT
Oonagh Ryan, ORA
923 East 3rd Street #105
Los Angeles, CA 90013
→ ora.la

BIRDHOUSE
Francisco Arredondo, North Arrow Studio
The Baker Center
3908 Avenue B, Classroom 307
Austin, TX 78751
→ northarrowstudio.com

JEWEL BOX
Joe Schneider and Michael Freeman, JAS Design Build
3600 Wallingford Avenue N
Seattle, WA 98103
→ jasdesignbuild.com

INSIDE ADDITION
Whitney Schrauth, SA+C Inc.
73 California Ave
Mill Valley, CA 94941
→ saandc.com

THE IT HOUSE
Linda Taalman, Taalman Architecture
2902 Rowena Avenue
Los Angeles, CA 90039
ithouseinc.com
→ taalmanarchitecture.com

THE WELL LIVING LAB
Christopher Strom and Isaiah Scharen, CSA
3308 Gorham Avenue
St. Louis Park, MN 55426
→ christopherstrom.com

LANEWAY CULTURE
Honomobo
8603 104 Street NW
Edmonton, AB, T6E 4G6, Canada
→ honomobo.com

THE WOODY CABINS
Marianne Borge
Oslo, Norway
marianneborge.com
→ woody.no

SLIM FIT
Ana Rocha
Lange Voorhout 102
2511 EK Den Haag, Netherlands
→ anarocha.nl

ACKNOWLEDGMENTS

I'd like to thank everyone who helped turn this idea into my first book.

It all started with the incomparable Tyrrell Mahoney of Chronicle Books, who listened to my pitch and saw the potential. From there, it was in the hands of my amazing and patient editor, Jennifer Thompson, of Princeton Architectural Press. I can't thank her enough for her steady direction and insight.

I'd like to thank my family, specifically Shearer Weigert, Martin Weigert, Betsy DiPrima, Laura Weigert, and Fabien Capeilleres, for always supporting and never questioning my meandering and unconventional career path.

Also, thank you to my friends, who stepped up in so many ways over the past year with inspiration, ideas, and motivation—not to mention food, drink, and free Casper-sitting. This includes Elliot and Andy Berndt, Andrea and Chris Flynn, Nancy and Tom King, Alison Littman, Elizabeth Malloy, Stephanie and Alan Pullman, Julie Stern, Kevin Whelan, and Christina Wilson. And last but not least, to my book club of the past twenty-plus years, some of the most compassionate and powerful women I know: thank you for always believing in me.

Thank you to Grace Kraaijvanger of the Hivery and my fearless 2024 Incubator cohort for a weekly infusion of confidence and empowerment as I fumbled my way through this project.

And finally, thank you to all the architects, designers, builders, homeowners, and ADU advocates who generously shared their stories, research, images, and precious time to help me tell this important story. It's a long list that includes Jared Basler, Robert Berry, Azadeh Garshasbi, Trisha Guido, Hisako Ichiki, Fiona Lennard, Ramiro Losada-Amor, Meredith Munger, Col Peterson, Oonagh Ryan, Loring Sagan, Ileana Schinder, Carrie Shores Diller, Whitney Schrauth, Bo Sundius, and Linda Taalman.

PHOTOGRAPHY AND ILLUSTRATION CREDITS

4: M. Stew Design

5: Andy MacPherson

6: Yoshihiro Makino

7: Courtesy of Honomobo

8–9: Adrià Goula

15: Eric Staudenmaier

17: Mark Constantini, *San Francisco Chronicle*, Polaris

20: Roof and Realm Builders

Lil' Red: Eric Staudenmaier

Garden Studio: Andy MacPherson Studio

Modern Craftsman: Julie Goldstone

Guest Pavilion: Adrià Goula

The Curve: Azadeh Garshasbi; Renderings: Saman Ramian

Space: Yoshihiro Makino: 64 (top), 65, 66, 70 (bottom), 72, 75; Yerin Mok: 63, 64 (bottom), 67, 68, 69, 70 (top), 71, 73, 74

Passage Island: Brit Kwasney

Alley Cat: Alyssa Lee Photography

Cloudview: M. Stew Design

Uplift: Janis Nicolay

Garage Mahal: Erin Kelleher

Radical Flexibility: Modern Granny Flat

Aging in Place: Ellyce Moselle Photography

Hidden Studio: Andy MacPherson Studio

Desert Retreat: Eric Staudenmaier

Birdhouse: Chase Daniel

Jewel Box: Jesse Young

Inside Addition: Courtesy of Whitney Schrauth

The IT House: Jesse Gillan

The Density Incentive: Atlas West Group

Laneway Culture: Courtesy of Honomobo

The Woody Cabins: Ivan Brodey & Jonas Adolfsen, All images copyright © Marianne Borge

Slim Fit: Christiane Wirth, Ana Rocha